Praise for *Landed Hong K*

"A long-awaited manual to the often difficult to understand Hong Kong property market. Dillon clearly summarizes every aspect of the market and its mix of new and archaic regulations that have resulted in the shape of our property market today. A must-have for everyone—whether tenant, landlord or long-time Hong Kong investor."

Allan Zeman
Chairman, Lan Kwai Fong Holdings Ltd.

"Owning your property is critical in Hong Kong, and a major commitment postponed for too long by many. Investing in property once you understand Hong Kong can provide handsome returns. *Landed Hong Kong*—written by a person who has done it himself—helps you keep your costs down, avoid pitfalls and recognize opportunities."

Paul Zimmerman
District Councillor, Pokfulam,
and CEO, Designing Hong Kong

"Dillon's book offers a wealth of up-to-date information on the context and specifics of Hong Kong's real estate environment. Especially useful are his clear and comprehensive lists of questions that simply must be asked before buying or renovating property in Hong Kong—guaranteed to reduce headaches!"

Richard Vuylsteke
President
American Chamber of Commerce in Hong Kong

"It is not Hong Kong property law that the newcomer finds perplexing, but Hong Kong property practice. *Landed* succinctly demystifies the issues and processes".

Hilary Cordell
Cordells
Specialists in Real Estate Law

"Hong Kong veteran Christopher Dillon gives readers the good, the bad and the ugly about buying and owning property. Dillon has done his homework, some of which involved paying tuition at the school of hard knocks, and his experiences are not only great stories but highly educational. I found the first edition of *Landed Hong Kong* invaluable when our company bought its office in Central in 2010. This new, expanded edition builds on strong foundations to provide a wealth of new insights about the Hong Kong property roller coaster."

Mark L. Clifford
Author of *The Greening of Asia: The Business Case for Solving Asia's Environmental Emergency*

"*Landed* won't make Hong Kong real estate any less expensive, but it is guaranteed to eliminate a lot of the guesswork, some of the cost and a large amount of the pain of being your own landlord."

David O'Rear
Chief Economist,
The Hong Kong General Chamber of Commerce

LANDED
HONG KONG

Christopher Dillon

For the next generation of Hong Kong homeowners

CONTENTS

ACKNOWLEDGEMENTS

I am grateful to the following people for sharing their time, expertise and contacts: Dr. Robert Collins, Doris Castagno, Bruce Grill, Grzegorz Laszczyk, Francis Lee, Rickie Lo, Marty Merz, Jonathan Sharp, Idalina Silva and Carrie Tan.

I would also like to thank the Canadian Academy of Independent Scholars for their support.

Photo credits

The author's photo is by Idalina Silva. All other photos were taken by the author.

PREFACE

Landed: The expatriate's guide to buying and renovating property in Hong Kong was written in 2008 after I purchased an office, an apartment and half of a floor in a factory building. There were no English-language books explaining how to buy property in Hong Kong, so I wrote one in the hope my experience would help others.

In 2010, I wrote *Landed: The guide to buying property in Japan.* Unlike the first volume, the Japan book was written before I had purchased property. As a result, I broadened my research: I interviewed architects, builders and agents. I met and wrote case studies about foreigners who had successfully bought and built property in Japan. I read newspapers and trade magazines to learn about trends shaping the market. And I scoured academic journals for practical information about subjects ranging from asbestos to zoning.

The second book included several new features. I added end notes and a "Useful information" chapter for readers who wanted additional resources, and a "Risk factors" chapter that highlighted several concerns, including Japan's troubled nuclear industry. Despite these changes, I retained a focus on clear, concise writing so that the book would be as accessible and useful as possible.

I continued that model in *Landed China* (2013) and in *Landed Global* (2014), and added several refinements. I shortened the name, had the cover and interior redesigned to reflect the fact that *Landed* was now a series and began producing ebooks.

All of these improvements continue in the second edition of *Landed Hong Kong*, which is nearly three times the length of its predecessor. *Landed Hong Kong* features new material, including a chapter about the New Territories and village houses, and information about buying a home off the plan. This edition also explains the special stamp duty and buyer's stamp duty that took effect in 2012, as well as the Minor Works Control System that was introduced in 2010.

Finally, *Landed Hong Kong* includes lessons that I have learned selling property, serving on the board of a management committee and dealing with unauthorized building works.

A lot has changed since the first edition of this book was published, but one thing remains constant. I hope *Landed Hong Kong* helps you make informed, profitable and satisfying decisions about real estate in Hong Kong.

INTRODUCTION

Landed Hong Kong was written for the general reader who is ready to buy a home or an investment property. Hong Kong has many persuasive real estate agents, so I have omitted the sales pitch.

This book also contains information and resources that will be helpful for tenants, for readers who are contemplating a real estate purchase or investment, and for anyone who is curious about one of the world's most distinctive and expensive property markets.

Hong Kong uses the metric system, but real estate continues to be measured in square feet, so both systems are used in *Landed Hong Kong*. All measurements refer to net salable area unless otherwise specified.

American English is used throughout this book. That includes spelling, style and the use of words like "elevator" instead of "lift."

Unless otherwise noted, all dollar figures are in Hong Kong dollars. The Hong Kong dollar is pegged to its American counterpart at HK$7.75–$7.85 = US$1.00. Property prices in Hong Kong fluctuate rapidly and are included here for illustrative purposes only.

Finally, *Landed Hong Kong* includes descriptions of laws that shape Hong Kong's real estate market. These descriptions are for background information only and are not legal advice.

BUYING BASICS

THE BUYING PROCESS

The first step in the buying process is to determine how much money you want to spend. If you are paying cash, this is easy. If you are using a mortgage, consult several lenders and learn how much you can borrow. Stress-test your borrowing assumptions to include higher interest rates, a property market downturn and other negative influences.

When you have a total budget, deduct the agent's commission, stamp duty and incidental costs, such as renovations, temporary accommodations during the move, moving expenses, legal fees and new furniture. Now you have a number—or a range of numbers—that you can use to shop for a home.

Choices

When you browse the listings, you will see several trends. In general:

- Detached houses cost more than town houses, which cost more than apartments.

- Hong Kong Island is more expensive than Kowloon, which is more expensive than the New Territories.

- New homes are more expensive than old ones. However, older homes sometimes have a higher efficiency ratio, which is the ratio between gross and salable floor area.

- Apartments on high floors are more expensive than units on low floors. High floors are quieter, have better air quality—particularly in congested neighborhoods—and often have superior views.

- Water views are auspicious and are preferable to hillside or city views. Homes that overlook a graveyard sell at a discount.

- Apartment blocks built above Mass Transit Railway stations are popular. With the exception of luxury homes like those on the Peak or in Shek O, long commutes reduce prices.

▲ Proximity to prestigious schools increases prices.

▲ Swimming pools, gyms, clubhouses and shuttle bus services add to the price of a home and to the monthly management fee.

The following prices were gathered from real estate listings in June 2015. They have almost certainly changed since then, but the relationship between the location, the size and the age of the homes is fairly constant. With a budget of $20 million you could buy:

▲ A 500-square-foot, sea-view apartment in an eight-year-old building on the waterfront in Tsim Sha Tsui

▲ A 600-square-foot apartment in a two-year-old building in Causeway Bay

▲ An 800-square-foot apartment in a 14-year-old building in Wanchai

▲ A 1,200-square-foot apartment in a 57-year-old building in Causeway Bay

▲ A 1,300-square-foot apartment in a 22-year-old building overlooking a graveyard in Pokfulam

▲ A 1,700-square-foot apartment in an eight-year-old building in Discovery Bay

▲ A 1,700-square-foot, 20-year-old house in Sai Kung

Purchasing a pre-owned property

1. You find a suitable property, usually with the help of a real estate agent. The agent may ask you to sign a document ("Form 4: Estate Agency Agreement for Purchase of Residential Properties in Hong Kong," available from the Estate Agents Authority's Website) appointing her to represent you in the purchase.

2. You inspect the property and its surroundings.

3. You and the vendor agree on a price for the property and other sale terms. The negotiation can be conducted with help from your respective agents.

4. Your real estate agent gives you a copy of the Land Registry search, which lists the property's address, its current and previous owners as well as any outstanding statutory orders, lawsuits, mortgages or other encumbrances.

5. You and the vendor sign a provisional sale and purchase (S&P) agreement and you give the vendor or his solicitor 3%–5% of the purchase price as a deposit. You and the vendor exchange proof of identity, typically Hong Kong identity cards. If the vendor or purchaser is a company, the corporate representative will also provide a copy of the company's business registration certificate.

The provisional S&P agreement is a standard form provided by the real estate agent. You write in the terms of the sale, including the purchase price, completion date and commission rates. After the S&P agreement is signed, if you fail to complete the purchase, you forfeit your deposit and must pay the real estate agent's commission. Similar penalties apply to the vendor, should he fail to complete the sale. Sample provisional S&P agreements and Land Registry searches are available on the Estate Agents Authority's Website. Consider taking out insurance on the property at this point.

You should ask the vendor and his agent if the vendor has negative equity in the property (i.e., the sale price is less than the outstanding mortgage loan). If there is negative equity, the provisional S&P agreement and formal S&P agreement should specify that any money you pay for the property is retained by the vendor's solicitor until the vendor can prove that the outstanding mortgage loan is less than the balance of the purchase price. This protects you if the vendor fails to discharge the mortgage before the sale is completed.

6. You appoint a solicitor to represent you.

7. Two weeks later, you sign a formal S&P agreement, which is normally prepared by the vendor's solicitor, and pay the vendor or his solicitor an additional 5%–7% of the purchase price, bringing your total deposit to 10%. This is usually done at your solicitor's office. If you are buying residential property, you now pay stamp duty, which officially registers the transaction with the government.[1]

8. The vendor's solicitor gives the deed for the property to your solicitor. Your solicitor confirms that the vendor has the right to sell the property; that the deed accurately describes the property; and that all outstanding mortgages, unpaid government rates and other liabilities are properly accounted for. The vendor's solicitor answers your solicitor's questions about the deed and the property, and clarifies any outstanding issues such as pending lawsuits. It is the vendor's responsibility to prove good title for the property, and your solicitor will continue to ask questions until he is satisfied or advises you to consider abandoning the purchase. During this time, your solicitor contacts your bank to arrange a mortgage deed if you are taking out a loan.

9. Your solicitor prepares an assignment, which formally transfers ownership of the property from the vendor to you.

10. The vendor's solicitor reviews and approves the assignment.

11. Thirty to 60 days after signing the provisional S&P agreement, you complete the transaction.

   ▲ You inspect the property to ensure it is as described in the S&P agreement and any fittings or fixtures included in the sale are in place.

   ▲ You sign the assignment and the mortgage deed, if necessary.

   ▲ Your solicitor completes an accounting of any outstanding charges or prepayments, such as government rates, management fees or deposits owed to tenants. These items are added to or deducted from the purchase price, which you pay to your solicitor along with the solicitor's fees and any amount not covered by the mortgage loan.

⚠ If you are buying commercial or industrial property, you now pay stamp duty.[2]

⚠ Your solicitor registers the assignment and new and discharged mortgages, if necessary, at the Land Registry.[3]

⚠ You pay the real estate agent's commission.

12. You take possession of the property.

Confirmors

When Hong Kong's property market is buoyant, speculators become more active. A common technique is for confirmor "A" to sign a provisional S&P agreement to buy a property from vendor "B" and arrange for a longer-than-usual completion date.

During the period between the signing of the provisional S&P agreement and the completion of the sale, "A" (the confirmor) sells the property to sub-purchaser "C" for a higher price. The confirmor usually purchases a property with the express purpose of flipping it, and there can be more than one confirmor between the initial vendor and the ultimate buyer.

Confirmor agreements can cause problems. Sub-purchasers often do not have an opportunity to inspect the property before they buy it, and the sub-purchaser is bound by the terms and conditions of the original S&P agreement between the vendor and the confirmor. The sequence of payments between the buyers and sellers needs to be carefully coordinated and if the confirmor is unable to complete the sale, the sub-sale may be delayed or the sub-purchaser may be unable to buy the property.

If a real estate agent represents the vendor and confirmor in the original sale and also represents the confirmor and sub-purchaser in a sub-sale, the agent must disclose to each of the parties any commissions receivable from the others.

In August 2010, the Hong Kong government banned confirmor transactions on uncompleted properties.

Failure to complete

The penalties for failing to complete a sale depend on who aborts the transaction and at which stage they abort it.

For example, if, after signing a provisional S&P agreement, the vendor refuses to sell the property, the vendor pays the buyer twice the amount of the buyer's original deposit, but only if this is specified in the provisional S&P agreement. The agreement is then canceled.

If the purchaser refuses to buy the property after signing a provisional S&P agreement, the buyer loses her original deposit and may have to pay the vendor compensation. The agreement is then canceled and the vendor can sell the property to a third party.

If the vendor refuses to sell the property after signing a formal S&P agreement, the vendor refunds all of the buyer's money and the buyer may sue the vendor for compensation. The amount of compensation will depend on the amount of money the buyer lost, typically as a result of buying a home in a rising market. The agreement is then canceled.

If the purchaser refuses to buy the property after signing a formal S&P agreement, the buyer may lose all of her deposit money and the vendor may sue for compensation. The amount of compensation will depend on the amount of money the vendor lost, typically as a result of selling the home at a discount. The agreement is then canceled and the vendor can sell the property to a third party.

REAL ESTATE AGENTS

The operation of real estate agencies in Hong Kong is governed by the Estate Agents Ordinance (Cap. 511) and regulated by the Estate Agents Authority (EAA), which is a statutory body established in 1997.

Agencies

At the end of February 2015, Hong Kong had 3,196 licensed real estate agencies. This includes the biggest multinational firms, a handful of large local companies, medium-sized niche players and one- and two-person operations.

Although categories overlap, the multinationals generally focus on large transactions, such as en bloc (whole building) sales, real estate investment trusts (REITS), advisory services and development projects. Firms in this category, such as Colliers International, Jones Lang LaSalle and Knight Frank, also handle houses and high-end apartments.

The larger homegrown companies include Centaline, Midland and Ricacorp. These firms have many branches throughout Hong Kong and handle sales and rentals of residential, commercial and industrial property. They operate bilingual Websites and have strong distribution capabilities, making them a good choice for owners wanting to list a property for sale.

The niche players tend to be smaller and focused on a specific market segment. Chartersince, for instance, is active in office rentals and sales. Smaller companies generally make up for their lack of size by offering deep knowledge of a specific neighborhood or market segment. They can also provide more flexible, personal service. On the other hand, large agencies offer the reassurance of a familiar brand, plus marketing, staff training and quality control programs.

Regardless of its size, each real estate agency's office must be managed by a person holding an estate agent's license.

Agents

Hong Kong had 35,587 licensed real estate agents at the end of February 2015. About 19,000 of those were salespeople, while the balance were licensed estate agents. A person holding an estate agent's license can work for themself or for another licensed estate agent. A salesperson must work for a licensed estate agent.[1]

To obtain an estate agent's license, applicants must be over 18 years of age, have completed form 5 (or its overseas equivalent) and pass a multiple-choice examination. Applicants must also be a "fit and proper person," which means they are not an undischarged bankrupt, a convicted criminal or suffering from mental illness, among other requirements.[2]

According to the EAA's practice guide, an agent's business card should include her license number. Agents are also expected to comply with the Personal Data (Privacy) Ordinance (Cap. 486) when collecting personal information about clients and prospects.

Agents typically receive a base salary of about $7,000 per month and split sales commissions with the agency that employs them. As a result, agents are under considerable pressure to close deals.

Agents are supposed to follow the EAA's practice circulars and code of ethics. The latter states that agents and salespeople should "protect and promote the interests of their clients, carry out the instructions of their clients in accordance with the estate agency agreement and act in an impartial and just manner to all parties involved in the transaction."

In practical terms, that means the agent should disclose conflicts of interest, conduct and provide buyers with a copy of the Land Registry search report and accurately convey information to clients and counterparties. However, penalties for failing to meet these standards are minor. Warnings, week-long license suspensions or fines of a few thousand dollars are common. From a client's perspective, it is better to conduct your own due diligence—on the agent, the property, the counterparty and the transaction—than to trust the system to look after your interests.

The quality of Hong Kong's real estate agents varies. I have worked with agents who took the time to understand my needs, helped me find suitable property and resolved potentially deal-breaking problems. Agents with the right attitude and skills are a valuable resource. Unfortunately, this level of service and competence is not universal.

Under the Estate Agents Ordinance, agents in Hong Kong do not need a Hong Kong agent's license to sell property that is outside Hong Kong. However, these agents are required to state in their ads, brochures and letters and accounts that they are not licensed to deal in property located in Hong Kong.

Finding and hiring an agent

Recommendations from friends and colleagues are a good place to start when searching for an agent. Follow this up with a visit to the Estate Agents Authority Website, where you can confirm that the agent is licensed and review the agent's disciplinary record for the past two years.

To get the best out of your agent, be an informed, educated consumer. Start by understanding the local market, which will allow you to ask questions and determine how much—or how little—the agent knows. If you get vague, evasive or incorrect answers, it may be time to find another agent.

Knowing your budget and schedule, as well as your preferred location, features, size and other requirements, and communicating this information clearly to the agent, demonstrates that you are a serious buyer. Tell the agent what is essential and where you can compromise. This approach saves everybody time and reduces the likelihood that the agent will show you homes that don't meet your needs.

Commissions

The buyer and seller pay 1% of the purchase price to their respective agents, and Hong Kong law allows one agent to act for both the buyer and seller, which is known as dual agency. Agents who belong to the Royal Institute of Chartered Surveyors are prohibited by RICS guidelines from representing both parties. For rentals, the tenant and landlord each pay half of one month's rent.

Discounted commissions can be negotiated—the rates listed here are not specified in the Estate Agents Ordinance—and buyers do not pay a real estate agent's commission when they purchase a property directly from a developer.

Note that if one agent shows you a property, and you buy the property using a second agent, the first agent can sue you for her lost commission. This also applies if the agent shows you a property and you subsequently buy the same property from the vendor without using an agent.[3]

Agency agreements can be exclusive or nonexclusive. They are typically valid for three months, but this is negotiable.

HONG KONG'S LEGAL SYSTEM

Hong Kong's legal system is unique. As a former British colony, Hong Kong uses the common law system found in England, the Commonwealth countries and the United States. Common law is supplemented by local legislation, and traditional Chinese law has been used in the New Territories since Britain leased it from China in 1898. On July 1, 1997, the Basic Law took effect when Hong Kong reverted to Chinese sovereignty.

Arbitration and mediation

The Hong Kong government encouraged the city's development as an international arbitration and mediation hub with the enactment of the Arbitration Ordinance (Cap. 609) and the Mediation Ordinance (Cap. 620), which came into effect in 2011 and 2013, respectively. Hong Kong has many skilled arbitrators and mediators, and arbitration awards made in Hong Kong are enforceable in over 140 jurisdictions.

The Basic Law

Under the Basic Law (www.basiclaw.gov.hk), the Hong Kong Special Administrative Region has a high degree of autonomy and enjoys executive, legislative and independent judicial power. The Basic Law states that the laws in force in Hong Kong before 1997 will be maintained and Hong Kong's capitalist system and way of life will remain unchanged until 2047. The Basic Law also recognizes English as one of Hong Kong's official languages.

The guarantees in the Basic Law mean that—unlike Mainland China—Hong Kong has no foreign exchange controls or restrictions on the repatriation of capital, dividends, interest, profits or rental income. Furthermore, there are no restrictions on foreigners owning property in Hong Kong, although buyers who are not permanent residents of Hong Kong pay higher rates of stamp duty.

Courts

Hong Kong's judiciary is recognized as being independent and free from government interference. The city's courts and tribunals operate in English and Chinese, and the Court Language Service provides interpretation services and certifies translations. The Bailiff Section serves summonses and other legal documents, and enforces court orders, including writs of possession, which landlords use to evict occupants and recover premises.

The following courts and tribunals deal with real estate–related issues.

The Court of Final Appeal
The Court of Final Appeal is Hong Kong's highest appellate court. It hears criminal and civil cases from the High Court.

The High Court
The High Court comprises the Court of Appeal and the Court of First Instance.

The Court of Appeal hears appeals on civil and criminal matters from the Court of First Instance, the District Court and the Lands Tribunal.

The Court of First Instance has unlimited jurisdiction on civil and criminal cases. It hears appeals from the Small Claims Tribunal and other lower courts and tribunals.

The District Court
The District Court hears civil disputes valued between $50,000 and $1 million, as well as criminal cases with sentences of less than seven years.

The Lands Tribunal
The Lands Tribunal handles applications for possession of premises; cases related to building management, compulsory sale, and compensation for expropriation; and appeals about ratable values and government rents.

The Small Claims Tribunal
The Small Claims Tribunal hears civil disputes valued at less than $50,000. Hearings are informal and litigants cannot be represented by lawyers.

The ICAC

The Independent Commission Against Corruption (ICAC) was formed in 1974 to fight corruption through a combination of law enforcement, prevention and education. Illegal business dealings and dishonest public officials can be reported directly to the ICAC, which also publishes guides on the effective operation of owners' corporations and related topics.

Lawyers

Hong Kong uses the British system, where front-line legal services such as conveyancing and preparing contracts are provided by solicitors, who are represented by the Law Society of Hong Kong. Barristers are appointed by solicitors to plead cases for clients in open court and do not deal directly with clients. Barristers are represented by the Hong Kong Bar Association.

Hong Kong has many highly qualified, bilingual solicitors. However, legal costs can be high. For simple conveyancing, you can negotiate the solicitor's fees in advance. Due to the extra paperwork involved, conveyancing charges for a mortgaged property are higher than those for a cash purchase.

An itemized list of the solicitor's fees and disbursements will be included in the completion statement, which specifies the amount the vendor must pay to complete the purchase of the property. Disbursements typically include courier and travel expenses; mortgage and assignment registration fees; and company, land and bankruptcy search fees.

Exercise caution if you receive "free" legal services from a developer or other third party, because the solicitor may be working for both you and your counterparty.

OWNERSHIP AND PROPERTY RIGHTS

In Hong Kong, all land except the ground under St. John's Cathedral in Central is owned by the Hong Kong government and leased to users. Under this policy, developers pay large, up-front premiums to acquire land. In the year ended March 31, 2015, the government sold 36 parcels of land totaling 34.3 hectares for $49.5 billion.[1]

Government land leases

The length of government land leases, which were known as Crown leases before 1997, varies widely.

▲ From 1849 to 1898, 999-year leases were used for lots on Hong Kong Island and parts of Kowloon. These leases remain in effect today.

▲ In the New Territories, leases were granted for 75 years starting from July 1, 1898, renewable for a further 24 years, less three days. See the "New Territories" chapter for details.

▲ In Hong Kong and Kowloon, most leases issued between 1899 and 1985 were for 75 years with an option to renew for another 75 years. Some leases signed during this period were for 99 years, with an option to renew for 99 years.

▲ Under the terms of Annex III of the Joint Declaration of the Government of the United Kingdom of Great Britain and Northern Ireland and the Government of the People's Republic of China on the Question of Hong Kong, leases signed between May 27, 1985, and June 30, 1997, expired on June 30, 2047.

▲ Under the Basic Law, leases signed after July 1, 1997, are for a period of 50 years.[2] Leases for gas stations and recreational property are for 21 years.

On June 30, 2047, the guarantee of "one country, two systems" that Hong Kong enjoys under the Basic Law will end, and the central government has not indicated how it will handle land leases after 2047. Uncertainty over 2047 is understandable, but it is worth noting that century-old Crown leases survived the resumption of Chinese sovereignty in 1997. Furthermore, in 2004 the Chinese constitution was amended to include the right to own private property. Finally, as Danny Gittings observes in his 2011 paper *What Will Happen to Hong Kong after 2047?*, the special administrative region could continue to operate under the terms of the Basic Law after 2047.[3]

Aside from the land under St. John's Cathedral, all land in Hong Kong is owned by the Hong Kong government.

The Land Registry

Hong Kong uses a deed registration system. At the heart of the system is the Land Registry, which is a public repository of sale and purchase agreements, assignments, deeds of mutual covenants, charges, mortgages and mortgage discharges, leases over three years in duration, certificates of compliance, occupancy permits, statutory orders, pending lawsuits, powers of attorney and legal instruments affecting land ownership. The fact that a document is in the Land Registry does not prove ownership. As Stephen Mau notes in *Property Law in Hong Kong: An Introductory Guide,* "The register does not make any representation concerning the ownership or the validity of documents that have been registered."[4]

Under the deed registration system, a solicitor reviews the title documents for a property every time a transaction takes place. After the solicitor has reviewed the documents, she forms an opinion about who owns the property. As the solicitor's opinion is based on her interpretation of the title documents, that opinion can be challenged in court. It is not unusual for a solicitor to recommend that a buyer abandon a purchase because of flaws in the title documents. If you consider a 20-year-old apartment complex comprising several 40-story towers built on lots purchased from several owners that were originally part of a 150-year-old government lease, it's easy to see how complex title documents can become and how disputes can arise.

Common title problems include mismatched names or signatures; missing documents; discrepancies in the property's description; missing or invalid powers of attorney; and illegible government leases.

Hong Kong's deed registration system differs from the title registration system used in other jurisdictions, such as Singapore and Australia. Under the title registration system, which is also known as the Torrens system, ownership of the property only has to be proven once, when the property is entered into a central registry. The title registration system saves time, money and uncertainty.

In 2004, the Hong Kong government enacted the Land Title Ordinance (Cap. 585), which will convert the deed registration system to a title registration system. Despite the passage of more than a decade, Hong Kong continues to use the deed registration system.

Ownership structures

In Hong Kong, property can be owned by permanent residents of Hong Kong, by nonpermanent residents and by nonresidents. Property can be owned by trusts, by Hong Kong–registered companies and by offshore companies. In the New Territories, property is owned by traditional Chinese institutions such as *Tsos* and *Tongs*.

Hong Kong also allows joint ownership of property. The two most common forms of joint ownership are joint tenancy—where each owner is entitled to the whole property, rather than an undivided share of the property—and tenancy in common, where each owner has an undivided share in the property.

When one owner in a joint tenancy dies, his share of the property passes to the other owner or owners. When one tenant in common dies, his share of the property forms part of his estate and passes to his heirs according to the terms of his will.

What you are buying

In Hong Kong, the vast majority of the population lives in multi-unit apartment blocks. Likewise, most of the city's retail, office and industrial space is in multi-unit buildings. In these buildings, each owner has a share in the land together with the exclusive right to use the unit that he has purchased. The relationship between owners is explained in a deed of mutual covenant, which applies to all owners. The deed of mutual covenant identifies common areas in the building and addresses rights of way, owners' meetings, building management, usage restrictions and related issues.

The use of multi- and single-unit buildings is also controlled by the terms of the government land lease, by the occupation permit issued by the Buildings Department and by the outline zoning plan for the area.

Zoning

Hong Kong has two zoning categories. The first is outline zoning plans that show the land uses and development restrictions for individual planning areas. Areas are classified as residential, commercial, industrial, green belt, open space, government/institution/community or other specified purposes. Each zone has a schedule of notes showing the uses that are always permitted (Column 1 uses) and other uses that require the prior permission of the Town Planning Board (Column 2 uses).

The second category is development permission area plans, which provide interim planning and development guidance for rural areas in the New Territories until detailed outline zoning plans are prepared. Development permission area plans include notes showing Column 1 and 2 uses.

Some outline zoning plans allow mixed uses, such as commercial operations in industrial buildings and dwellings in commercial buildings. Hong Kong has numerous developments that are built above a Mass Transit Railway station, include shops and restaurants on a podium level and have multiple residential towers above. Union Square, which incorporates Kowloon Station, the Elements shopping mall, the International Commerce Center and 15 residential towers, is one example.

Hong Kong's high density makes for some interesting zoning decisions. In Pokfulam, this liquefied petroleum gas storage facility is less than 200 meters from a luxury residential development.

Zoning plays a key role in a property's price. Within a few hundred meters, industrial property will sell at $5,000 per square foot ($54,000 per square meter), commercial property at $10,000 per square foot and residential property at $20,000 per square foot.

A building's zoning can be changed if the owner applies to the government, obtains approval and pays a land conversion premium. Often, the premium is so large as to make the process uneconomical. Using a building for an unauthorized purpose—for example living in a factory—can theoretically result in eviction and large fines.

BUILDING MANAGEMENT

Most of Hong Kong's population lives in apartment blocks that have common areas, like lobbies, and shared infrastructure, such as plumbing and electrical systems. In most buildings, common elements are managed by an owners' corporation, a management committee and a property management company.

Deed of mutual covenant

The management and operation of multi-unit buildings are governed by a deed of mutual covenant (DMC), which is an agreement that is signed by the developer, the first management company and the initial people or companies buying units in the building. DMCs are signed shortly after the building is completed and are binding on all subsequent owners.

DMCs cover high-level issues, such as the procedures for forming an owners' corporation and hiring a management company. They also address practical concerns, such as whether residents can have dogs or operate a business from their apartment, which parts of the building are common areas and house rules for renovations.

DMCs are registered with the Land Registry and may not contravene the provisions of the Building Management Ordinance (Cap. 344).[1] DMCs can be complex, 200-page documents, which some new buildings post online.

Operating entities

Owners' corporations
Buildings in Hong Kong that have more than one owner usually have an owners' corporation (OC). While there is no legal requirement to form an OC, it provides a predictable, relatively simple framework for managing common problems.[2]

The Building Management Ordinance regulates the establishment, operation and rights and responsibilities of OCs, which are independent statutory bodies that are registered with the Land Registry. OCs can sue, be sued, collect management fees and pass resolutions that are legally binding on management committees and individual apartment owners.

OCs are required to hold annual general meetings and keep meeting minutes and other records (see below). OCs are also responsible for the control and management of common parts of the building, including:

▲ General repairs and maintenance

▲ Implementing government work orders

▲ Enforcing the DMC

▲ Employing building management staff

▲ Financial management

▲ Taking out building insurance

▲ Fire safety

▲ Security and crime prevention

▲ Environmental hygiene

▲ Complying with the Code of Practice on Building Management and Maintenance[3]

OCs are expected to keep a range of records and documents, including building plans; drawings and schematics for the drainage, water supply, fire services and electricity supply and lighting systems; and contracts for the installation and maintenance of water pumps, elevators, generators, air-conditioning and other systems and services.

Owners may form a mutual aid committee or an owners' committee, rather than an OC. However, these committees lack the legal powers of an OC.[4]

Management committees

OCs form a management committee—with a chairman, secretary and treasurer—that acts on behalf of all of the building's owners. Committees must meet at least every three months. Buildings with fewer than 50 apartments must have a minimum of three committee members, buildings with 50–100 units must have at least seven members and those with more than 100 units must have nine or more members.

Under the Building Management Ordinance, a management committee's chairman, vice-chairman, secretary and treasurer may receive a monthly allowance of up to $1,200. However, management committee members are often volunteers.

Committees operate bank accounts; buy and approve the purchase of products and services; pay for insurance, utilities and government rent; and produce annual budgets and prepare financial statements. In buildings with more than 50 units, the financial statements must be audited.

In addition, committees set and collect management fees from owners. These fees pay for the building's day-to-day operation and may be used for a contingency fund to cover burst pipes and other emergencies. Committees have the power to make special assessments for major expenditures, such as replacing a building's roof.

If owners are unhappy with the management committee's performance, they can call a special meeting where they can vote to have the committee dissolved.

Committees may employ staff, such as security guards and cleaners. However, most committees hire a property management company to provide security, maintenance and cleaning services.

Property management companies

Small and medium-sized buildings are usually managed by small property management companies with a portfolio of similar properties. Big complexes often employ large companies that are part of a conglomerate. The quality and sophistication of the services vary. Some larger companies are ISO-certified and provide polished, professional services. Smaller companies typically offer more basic services.

Staff of management companies are not well paid. Employees switch jobs frequently and it's not unusual to find security guards dozing at night. It can be difficult to recruit and retain employees if inexpensive accommodations are not available nearby and staff face a long commute to work.

Practical considerations

Effective property management can have a dramatic effect on your quality of life. Attentive security guards, reliable elevators, clean common areas and compliance with the house rules all contribute to a pleasant living environment. Good management can also influence your property's value. A 2008 study in Sweden found a 13% price difference between a well-maintained 40-year-old property and an unmaintained dwelling of the same age.[5]

Management fees can range from 5%–20% of an apartment's monthly rent and are calculated on a per square foot or per unit basis. In buildings with a private road, clubhouse, pool, gym or other facilities that require extra staff or regular maintenance, management fees can be significant. Overhauling these facilities can result in a special assessment of hundreds of thousands of dollars per apartment.

Management fees, which are also charged for parking spaces, can be paid directly to the management company or to the OC. The latter is preferable, as management companies sometimes go bankrupt.

Resolutions passed by OCs are legally binding on the building's owners. However, owners sometimes refuse to pay for their share of a renovation project. These disputes frequently end up in court, delaying a project for months or years.

Many owners skip annual meetings and ignore management committee notices, preferring to trust in the common sense and stinginess of their neighbors. This can lead to abuse in poorly governed management committees.

Unless the building has a large number of expatriate owners, most management committee and OC meetings are conducted in Cantonese. Owners who do not speak Cantonese can send a friend to act on their behalf or give the chairman a proxy to vote for them.

Items discussed in these meetings are usually straightforward, such as landscaping and minor repairs. Renovations, compliance with government regulations and other potentially expensive issues are also debated in these meetings, so it is a good idea to attend or read the reports that are issued after the meeting.

The interests and priorities of the building's owners are reflected in the OC's decisions. For example, if a tightfisted landlord owns a large proportion of the building, it may be difficult to get repairs done. If you are retired and live in a building with many families, you may have to pay for the installation and maintenance of playground facilities that you don't use.

OCs respond to economic forces. When the property market is depressed, few OCs want to spend money on improvements, despite the fact that this is often when contractors are idle and less expensive.

Inspections and maintenance

Owners' corporations are responsible for ensuring that inspections and maintenance take place regularly and that their buildings remain safe. This includes fixing cracked walls, spalling cement, and rusted water pipes and leaks, among other issues. Owners who fail to repair these problems can be held jointly and severally responsible for any resulting damage.

Building inspections
In 2012, the government introduced the Mandatory Building Inspection Scheme (MBIS). Under the MBIS, each year the Buildings Department selects 2,000 residential buildings that are more than 30 years old and over three stories tall. Owners of selected buildings receive a statutory order that requires them to hire a registered inspector to check the building and a registered contractor to make any necessary repairs. Owners who fail to comply can be prosecuted and

the Buildings Department can make the repairs and recover the costs, plus a surcharge, from the owners.[6]

The inspections focus on fire safety, the building's structural integrity, drainage and the presence of unauthorized building works. Fixing problems uncovered by the scheme can result in large bills. One estimate placed the cost per apartment at $68,000 for a 50-unit, 30-year-old building.[7]

In addition to making general repairs and removing unauthorized building works, the MBIS can interrupt the renovations you have arranged for your apartment. The MBIS also provides an opportunity for unscrupulous contractors, surveyors and engineers to fix prices and defraud owners. In 2014, residents of Garden Vista in Sha Tin received a maintenance bill for $260 million, or $350,000 per household.[8]

Electrical systems
Electrical installations of more than 100 amperes must be inspected, tested and certified every five years by a registered contractor. The contractor will issue a WR2 certificate, which the owner is required to send to the Electrical and Mechanical Services Department (EMSD).

Elevators
Owners are required to appoint a registered lift contractor to:

▲ Inspect, clean, oil and adjust the elevator once a month

▲ Test and examine safety equipment once a year

▲ Test the full load, overload device and the brake once every five years

Building owners must submit the contractor's certificate of examination to the EMSD within seven days, countersign the contractor's logbook after the repair work has been completed and report accidents immediately, in writing, to the EMSD, the contractor and the building's insurance company.[9]

Energy efficiency

The Buildings Energy Efficiency Ordinance (Cap. 610), which took effect in September 2012, requires that certain new and refurbished buildings meet standards set out in the Building Energy Code. The ordinance applies to the common areas of residential buildings and to the commercial portion of composite buildings (i.e., buildings that include commercial and residential elements). The commercial portions of composite buildings are also required to have an energy audit every 10 years.[10]

In the long term, the ordinance will help building owners save money through increased energy efficiency. In the short term, however, complying with the ordinance will cost money. In November 2014, the EMSD announced that it had successfully prosecuted its first case against owners who failed to comply with the ordinance.

Fire equipment

Owners are required to hire a registered fire service installation contractor to inspect the hose reels, extinguishers, alarm systems and automatic sprinkler systems at least once every 12 months. The Fire Services Department maintains a list of accredited contractors.[11]

Gas installations

Gas installations are checked every 18 months by Towngas, Hong Kong's monopoly supplier of piped gas.

Slopes and retaining walls

Owners are responsible for the safety and maintenance of slopes and retaining walls on their property and may also be responsible for slopes and retaining walls that are adjacent to their land. The responsibility for adjoining areas is normally specified in the land lease, but it can also come about because the owner has cut into an adjoining plot. The Lands Department operates the Slope Maintenance Responsibility Information System, an online directory that lists the parties responsible for maintaining registered slopes and retaining walls.

The engineer who designs the slope or retaining wall should prepare a manual that explains what maintenance activities are required and a schedule for conducting the work. If a manual does not exist, it can be created by the engineer supervising the maintenance, which usually occurs once a year. Owners are responsible for keeping records of inspections and remedial work.

Slope maintenance typically includes:

▲ Clearing debris, loose rock and undesirable vegetation from drainage channels and the slope surface

▲ Repairing or replacing cracked or damaged drainage channels and slope surfaces

▲ Unblocking drains and drainpipes

▲ Maintaining grass and other landscaping on the slope

▲ Repairing missing or damaged pointing in masonry walls

▲ Repairing leaky water mains and drainpipes[12]

Water pipes and drains
At a minimum, the Water Supplies Department recommends that building owners clean freshwater storage tanks every three months. Flush water tanks should be cleaned every six months. The department recommends that a plumber, surveyor or engineer inspects the building's plumbing every three months.[13] The building's drains, including ventilation pipes, should also be inspected regularly.

Windows
The Buildings Department also operates the Mandatory Window Inspection Scheme, which targets buildings that are more than 10 years old and over three stories tall. This program is similar to the Mandatory Building Inspection Scheme, which is explained above.

RISK FACTORS

This chapter outlines potential issues affecting real estate in Hong Kong, including economic, environmental, legal, political and property-specific concerns. These risks are summarized in the "Property Buyer's Checklist" at the end of the book.

Adverse possession

Under the Limitation Ordinance (Cap. 347), if a property is not used by its owner and another person has used it for at least 12 years without objection, the person using the property can claim ownership in court.

Several conditions must be met for a claim to succeed. The user must have had exclusive, continuous physical control of the property for the 12-year period. In addition, the user must possess the property publicly and without the owner's permission. Adverse possession can also apply to government-owned land after a 60-year period.

Adverse possession cases can be complicated in the New Territories, where owners frequently gave people verbal, not written, permission to use their land.

Air pollution

In October 2013, the World Health Organization (WHO) classified outdoor air pollution as carcinogenic. Air pollution also causes cardiovascular diseases, respiratory infections and chronic obstructive pulmonary diseases. Children are vulnerable, due to the immaturity of their respiratory systems, as are the elderly.

Hong Kong has a serious air pollution problem. In its 2014 midyear report, the non-governmental organization Clean Air Network observed that with just two exceptions, levels of nitrogen dioxide, suspended particulates, fine particulates, sulfur dioxide and ozone at 15 monitoring stations exceeded the annual guidelines set by the WHO. In the first six months of 2014, air pollution was estimated to have caused more than 1,400 premature deaths in Hong Kong.[1]

Research by the University of California at Los Angeles and the California Air Resources Board shows that people living near busy roads are exposed to much higher concentrations of fine particulates.[2] This is an issue in Hong Kong's narrow, congested streets, many of which are surrounded by tall buildings that trap pollutants.

In addition to being a health risk for the general population, air pollution has made Hong Kong less attractive to internationally mobile senior executives and knowledge workers, especially those with children. If the air pollution worsens, it could damage the city's economy, resulting in lower property prices, especially for the larger, more expensive homes that are popular with expatriates.

People and vehicles are in close proximity in Hong Kong, exacerbating the effects of noise and air pollution.

Aluminum wiring

Aluminum wiring is approved for use in certain applications in Hong Kong, according to the Code of Practice for the (Electricity) Wiring Regulations.

Aluminum wiring is safe, but it poses two problems. First, when aluminum is heated and cooled, it expands and contracts at a different rate than other metals, including copper, which is often used in the terminals of circuit breakers, light switches and wall outlets. Over time, heating and cooling can make a copper–aluminum connection loose, creating a fire hazard. Second, aluminum oxidizes. Aluminum oxide is an insulator that adds electrical resistance to aluminum–aluminum connections, causing heat buildup and creating a fire hazard. Both of these problems can be overcome with regular inspections and maintenance.

American citizenship

On July 1, 2014, the Foreign Account Tax Compliance Act (FATCA) took effect. FATCA requires financial institutions outside the United States to report information about accounts held by American taxpayers to the Internal Revenue Service. Some foreign banks have found the cost and effort of complying with these requirements to be excessive and have stopped serving American clients. Americans living in Mexico, Switzerland, Belgium and other countries have had their accounts unilaterally closed by their banks.

In October 2014, we conducted an informal telephone survey of eight mortgage lenders in Hong Kong. The banks varied in size and were headquartered in Mainland China, England, Hong Kong and the United States. Each of the banks said it would provide a mortgage to an American citizen living in Hong Kong, if her income was earned and reported in Hong Kong, she had a Hong Kong identity card and she met the bank's normal loan-to-value and income requirements.

Asbestos

Asbestos is a naturally occurring family of minerals prized for its tensile strength and resistance to heat, electricity and chemicals.

Inhaling asbestos fibers, however, causes lung cancer, mesothelioma, asbestosis and other diseases. The WHO notes that, "There is no evidence for a threshold for the carcinogenic effect of asbestos and that increased cancer risks have been observed in populations exposed to

very low levels." Cigarette smokers exposed to asbestos are more likely to develop lung cancer than nonsmokers.

The import, supply and use of asbestos and asbestos containing materials are banned in Hong Kong. Despite this ban, there is a substantial amount of "legacy" asbestos in roofs, canopies and unauthorized
building works. Asbestos in building materials is believed to pose a
low risk, unless the materials are cut or broken and asbestos fibers are
released into the air. This can occur when buildings are renovated and
demolished.

The Hong Kong Housing Authority, the body that operates the city's
public housing estates, banned the use of asbestos in 1984 and has
removed most of the asbestos from estates built before this date.

Owners whose premises contain asbestos—or may reasonably be sus-
pected to contain asbestos—must use a registered asbestos contractor
when removing the asbestos and give advance written notice to the
Environmental Protection Department of the date the work will start.
Under the Air Pollution Control Ordinance (Cap. 311), owners who fail
to meet these requirements are liable to a fine of up to $200,000 and
six months in jail. Asbestos waste is considered to be chemical waste
and must be properly disposed of by a registered contractor.[3]

China

On July 1, 1997, Hong Kong reverted to China, ending a colonial era
that began in 1842. Hong Kong has prospered since 1997, benefiting
from China's rapid growth and economic liberalization, and Beijing's
relatively light touch. However, Hong Kong's housing market does
face some China-related risks.

The first threat is economic. China influences every aspect of Hong
Kong's economy and a slowdown or a loss of confidence in China's
growth prospects could depress housing prices.

The second is policy related. Since 1997, there have been issues—
notably the proposed security legislation that saw 500,000 people
march in the streets on July 1, 2003, disputes over Mainland shoppers in Hong Kong, and Beijing's 2014 white paper and the subsequent

Occupy Central protests—where there has been discord between Hong Kong's people, its government and the central government. Issues like these influence public sentiment, and a more interventionist approach by Beijing or restrictions on Mainland residents' ability to visit and invest in Hong Kong could hurt property prices.

The third risk is 2047. While Article 120 of the Basic Law states that all land leases granted or renewed before June 30, 1997, will continue to be recognized, no one knows how Hong Kong will be administered after 2047. This question is pressing because 30-year mortgages will soon straddle 2047.

Environmental issues, such as air pollution from the Pearl River Delta (PRD), also pose a risk. However, the central government has made improving the environment a national priority and a growing number of low-value-added manufacturers are leaving the PRD in search of cheaper land and labor costs in other parts of China and Asia.

In 2014, the Occupy Central protests brought large portions of Hong Kong to a standstill.

Compulsory sale

At the end of 2014, private buildings completed before 1980 represented 32.7% of Hong Kong's domestic units, 13.9% of the office space, 36.0% of the commercial space and 39.8% of the industrial space.[4] Many of these properties are at or near the end of their useful lives. Units with defective titles, with untraceable owners or with owners who have died intestate are common. Redevelopment of old buildings is often impeded by a single owner who demands an excessive price for his unit.

The Land (Compulsory Sale for Redevelopment) Ordinance (Cap. 545) was introduced in 1999 to facilitate the redevelopment of old buildings. In general, if a person or persons own 90% of the undivided shares in a building, they can apply to the Lands Tribunal for a compulsory sale order. The applicant must show that the redevelopment is justified due to the property's age or condition and that the majority owner or owners have tried to acquire all the undivided shares in the building. If the identity of the owner who refuses to sell is known, the applicant is expected to try to resolve the impasse through mediation.

In 2010, the ordinance was amended to allow a compulsory sale when a person or persons own 80% of the undivided shares in a building, if any of the following conditions are met:

▲ The building has fewer than 10 units

▲ The building is over 50 years old

▲ The property is an industrial building that is more than 30 years old

Redeveloping property can be very profitable—especially when an old four-story walk-up is replaced with a new 20-story tower—and aggressive and illegal tactics are sometimes used to encourage owners to sell. This includes cutting off the building's water or electricity supply, subjecting owners to threatening phone calls and loud noises and obstructing access to the property.

Death

Despite Hong Kong's ultramodern skyline, superstition plays a large role in the city's real estate market.

Death in a home—particularly a gruesome murder or a suicide that has been covered in the media—can reduce a property's resale price and rental value by up to 50%. In extreme cases, it can even affect the value of adjacent apartments or entire buildings.

The Estate Agents Ordinance does not require agents to inform buyers that a high-profile death has occurred in a dwelling—although this information may be included in the property's Land Registry record—or that a residence is haunted. Buyers should ask the agent directly if there has been a murder or suicide in a home because agents are supposed to disclose this information if they are asked.[5]

In Cantonese, the number four is a homonym for death. Apartment buildings, offices, hotels and hospitals often omit any floor with a four in it, effectively making the 4th, 14th and 24th floors disappear. In a concession to Western superstition, some buildings also omit the 13th floor.

Many people make offerings to their ancestors during the annual Ching Ming (March/April), Yue Laan (August/September) and Chung Yeung (September/October) festivals. Offerings—which can include ceremonial banknotes minted by the Bank of Hell and paper models of Mercedes-Benz sedans—are usually burned at the graveside, which often results in hill fires. Gifts are also burned on the street or in the stairwells of apartment buildings.

Buyers avoid homes near funeral parlors, cemeteries and crematoria. Research by Yeung Yuen-ting found that Hong Kong homes with a cemetery view were subject to a "significant" price penalty. Yeung noted that the discount was greater when the property market was buoyant and in wealthy neighborhoods. She also found that there was little difference in the size of the penalty between homes with a full cemetery view and those with a partial view.[6]

During Ching Ming and Chung Yeung, traffic near cemeteries is congested and buses and minibuses are full, giving buyers another reason to avoid these areas.

Even if you are unconcerned about ghosts, a haunted property can be difficult to resell. Some entrepreneurs buy these homes and rent them to non-Chinese tenants, who are often less sensitive to the spirit world.

Defective design and construction

In Hong Kong, only a few companies have the resources to acquire the land and finance the design and construction of large apartment complexes. As a result, fly-by-night and under-capitalized developers are kept out of the market and modern residential buildings are generally well designed and constructed.

That's not to say that Hong Kong's apartment buildings are problem-free. For example, in 2012, the *South China Morning Post* reported more than 150 cases of windows spontaneously breaking in residential buildings including The Arch and The Harbourside in Kowloon, The Legend in Happy Valley and The Larvotto in Ap Lei Chau.[7] The Larvotto continued to experience glass-related problems as recently as June 2014. Windows falling from high-rise buildings can kill people and damage property, and individual apartment owners can be held legally responsible.[8]

Three-story homes in the New Territories erected under the Hong Kong government's Small House Policy are often developed by local entrepreneurs. The quality of these homes, especially dwellings built in the 1980s and 1990s, can be poor.

In the late 1990s, several public housing estates in the New Territories experienced problems with subsidence. Two estates in Sha Tin were demolished when they were found to have defective pilings.

Many industrial premises and Grade B and C office buildings built during the 1980s and 1990s were erected quickly using the cheapest materials available. Leaky walls and windows, spalling concrete and other problems are common.

Rusting steel rebar caused spalling in this concrete ceiling.

Expropriation

In Hong Kong, expropriation is known as resumption. It occurs when the government takes land or rights belonging to an individual for a public purpose.

Resumption is subject to the Lands Resumption Ordinance (Cap. 124). Land in Hong Kong is commonly resumed to build transportation infrastructure such as roads (Cap. 370) and rail lines (Cap. 519 and Cap. 276), for drainage projects (Cap. 446) and for the redevelopment of old buildings by the Urban Renewal Authority (Cap. 563).

Compared with many places, resumption in Hong Kong is transparent. There are established processes for valuing property and for notifying and compensating affected tenants and owners. A formal appeal mechanism is also available.

However, the government's resumption decisions can generate controversy. Critics complain that the Urban Renewal Authority displaces residents and shop owners and destroys the character of neighborhoods. For example, buildings on Lee Tung Street in Wanchai—which was better known as Wedding Card Street after the printing companies that operated there—were demolished in 2007 to make way for a redevelopment project by Hopewell Holdings and Sino Land.

Some tenants and owners want more compensation than they are offered by the government, while others simply don't want to move. In 2011, some 200 households were relocated from Tsoi Yuen Tsuen, a village in the New Territories that was in the path of a high-speed rail line between Hong Kong and Shenzhen. Resumption in the New Territories is complicated by the area's political structure and because residents who are officially recognized as indigenous villagers receive more compensation than residents who are classified as squatters.

There are variations in the way that resumption is handled in different parts of Hong Kong. These differences are explained in two guides produced by the Lands Department: Land Resumption and Compensation in the Urban Area and How to Receive Compensation for Private Land Resumed in the New Territories by the Government.

Falling objects

Most Hong Kong people live in high-rise towers, a situation that makes falling objects a regular—and lethal—occurrence. Between 1996 and 2012, an average of eight people died each year from falling objects.[9] From January 2007 to September 2009, police received more than 3,000 reports of falling items.[10] The actual number was higher, as not all incidents resulted in a police report.

The variety of falling items is astonishing: people, wardrobes, windowpanes, microwave ovens, televisions, bottles of acid, knives, sledgehammers, garbage and mattresses. Accidents, mischief, mental illness and suicide are common causes.

Falling objects can lead to criminal prosecution. Under the Summary Offenses Ordinance (Cap. 228), a person convicted of dropping an item from a building can be fined $10,000 and jailed for six months. If the incident involves a more serious offense, like dropping corrosive fluid, the police can prosecute the perpetrator under other ordinances.

Windows are one of the most common items to fall from buildings. The Buildings Department recommends that windows be maintained regularly and inspected by a qualified person every five years. In 2012, the Mandatory Window Inspection Scheme was introduced. See the "Building management" chapter for details.[11]

Falling debris can make a terrace or patio unusable. Accumulated garbage can also block drains and create a fire or hygiene hazard.

Fire

Two fires shaped modern Hong Kong. On Christmas Day 1953, a blaze destroyed the Shek Kip Mei shantytown in Kowloon, killing two people, leaving 53,000 homeless and leading to the creation of a public housing program that now provides homes for millions of people. On November 20, 1996, a spark from a welder's torch started a fire in an elevator shaft of the Garley Building in Kowloon that killed 40 people and injured 80. It was the deadliest peacetime fire in Hong Kong's history.

Regulations have been tightened several times since these tragedies, but Hong Kong's large number of tall buildings and high density make fire safety an ongoing concern. In addition, home buyers should note the following:

▲ From October to April each year, Hong Kong is prone to hill fires, many of which are accidentally started by grave sweepers. These can be deadly: five people died in a blaze in Pat Sing Leng in February 1996. They can also be large, like the fire that consumed 400 hectares of parkland near Tuen Mun in November 2006.

▲ Fires in industrial buildings have claimed many lives over the years. Blocked emergency exits and stairwells and the presence of chemicals and dangerous goods are often cited as contributing factors.

▲ As a result of bad planning and local politics, emergency vehicles cannot reach some village houses in the New Territories. In October 2012, two boys died in a house fire in Wing Hing Wai because the walls of neighboring homes extended into the road, blocking access by fire engines.

▲ Unauthorized building works, like the creation of open-plan kitchens, may violate fire regulations.

Fire safety in domestic buildings over three stories tall is mainly governed by the Fire Safety (Buildings) Ordinance (Cap. 572). The ordinance requires that domestic buildings have a fire hydrant and hose
reel system, a manual fire alarm and emergency lighting in common
areas. Domestic buildings are also required to have a means of escape,
fire-resistant construction and a means of access for firefighters and
rescue crews.[12]

The Fire Services Ordinance (Cap. 95) covers the Fire Services
Department's ability to enter and inspect buildings and issue fire hazard orders, the registration and certification of fire service equipment
and contractors, and related subjects.

In addition, the Buildings Department publishes the Code of Practice
for Fire Safety in Buildings, which includes design and construction
specifications.

Hill fires are common during the dry season and are often started by grave
sweepers burning offerings for their ancestors.

Floods, rain and typhoons

The southwest monsoon, monsoon troughs and typhoons produce heavy rain in Hong Kong during the summer months. Land–sea breeze convergence and passing frontal systems can also cause heavy rains during the cool season. Hong Kong's mean annual rainfall ranges from about 1,400 millimeters at Ping Chau in the northeast New Territories to more than 3,000 millimeters near Tai Mo Shan, Hong Kong's highest peak.

The Hong Kong Observatory operates a three-tier rainstorm warning system, where an amber alert corresponds to 30 millimeters of rainfall per hour, with red and black warnings indicating 50 and 70 millimeters per hour, respectively. Between 1992 and 2001, about 30 amber, five red and one black warnings were issued, on average, each year.[13] The observatory also issues special announcements about flooding in the northern New Territories.

Hong Kong typically experiences six to seven typhoons each year. During a typhoon, strong winds can topple trees, blow out windows and knock down signs and other structures. Hong Kong uses a five-stage typhoon warning system.

▲ Signal 1 is raised when a tropical cyclone is within 800 kilometers of Hong Kong.

▲ Signal 3 indicates that strong winds are expected or are blowing in Hong Kong with sustained speeds of 41–62 kilometers per hour (kph) and gusts that may exceed 110 kph.

▲ Signal 8 indicates that gale or storm force winds are expected or blowing in Hong Kong, with sustained speeds of 63–117 kph and gusts that may exceed 180 kph. When a Signal 8 is raised, businesses and schools close and most nonessential activities stop.

▲ Signal 9 means that gale or storm force wind is increasing or expected to increase significantly.

▲ Signal 10 indicates hurricane force winds are expected or blowing with sustained wind speeds of 118 kph and gusts that may top 220 kph.

Low atmospheric pressure and high winds associated with typhoons produce powerful storm surges. About 10,000 fishermen drowned in a 1906 typhoon, with a similar number of fatalities in 1937, when the maximum sea level (high tide plus storm surge) reached an estimated six meters. More recently, in 1962 Typhoon Wanda produced a sea level of 3.96 meters and claimed 183 lives, while the sea level rose 3.53 meters during fatality-free Typhoon Hagupit in 2008. The observatory notes that Tolo Harbor is particularly susceptible to storm surges.[14]

The Drainage Services Department maintains a list of flooding "blackspots," which it ranks from 1 to 4, with 1 indicating a minor nuisance or an affected area of less than 2,500 square meters and 4 affecting more than 100 hectares or creating serious social and economic disruption. Since 1989, the department has spent $24 billion, reduced the number of blackspots from 120 to 11 and eliminated all of the category 4 blackspots.[15] As of November 2014, the remaining blackspots were in North District (2), Yuen Long (1), Tuen Mun (1), Tai Po (3), Yau Tsim Mong (1), Southern District (2) and Wanchai (1). A map and additional details are available on the department's Website.

Floods are most common during the summer months.

Foreign exchange risk

On October 17, 1983, Hong Kong introduced a currency board system that pegged the Hong Kong dollar to the United States dollar at
US$1.00 = HK$7.80. Since 2005, the rate has floated between HK$7.75
and HK$7.85. When the rate reaches HK$7.75, Hong Kong's de facto
central bank, the Hong Kong Monetary Authority, offers to buy U.S.
dollars.

The currency board system was introduced to stop capital outflows
and reverse a drop in the value of the Hong Kong dollar during ne-
gotiations for the return of Hong Kong to China. Previously, Hong
Kong used the silver standard (1863–1935), a sterling link (1935–72),
a U.S. dollar link (1972–74) and a free float (1974–83). During the
decade when the exchange rate floated, it ranged from HK$4.965 to
HK$9.600.[16]

Bankers, politicians, academics and pundits have regularly called for
the U.S. dollar peg to be replaced with a free float or with a link to the
yuan or to a basket of currencies. With equal regularity, these suggestions have been dismissed by the Hong Kong government.

The peg has withstood periods of intense pressure during the Asian
and global financial crises of 1997–98 and 2008–09, respectively.
However, China's moves to make the yuan fully convertible, concerns
about Hong Kong importing inflation and asset bubbles from the
United States and the end of "one country, two systems" in 2047 all
suggest that the current peg system will be amended.

Fraud, scams and gray areas

Hong Kong is a laissez-faire market, and the rule of law remains one of
the city's strengths. However, bodies such as the Consumer Council,
the Sales of First-hand Residential Properties Authority and the
Estate Agents Authority have limited enforcement and disciplinary
powers. As a result, buyers should be skeptical, ask questions and take
little for granted.

Common real estate frauds—such as vendors selling property that
they do not own and people selling one home to multiple buyers—are

relatively rare in Hong Kong. If this happens, it is usually at the signing of a provisional sale and purchase (S&P) agreement, when the buyer pays an initial deposit to the vendor. In general, real estate agents do a good job of ensuring that the vendor and transaction are legitimate, but it is wise to ensure that the name on the vendor's identity card, the name on the S&P agreement and the check payee's name are identical.

Infrastructure projects

Hong Kong has several multibillion-dollar projects at different stages of development. For example, Airport Authority Hong Kong is now planning a third runway and between 2016 and 2018 the Hong Kong–Zhuhai–Macau Bridge and the Tuen Mun–Chek Lap Kok Link will enter service.

The Mass Transit Railway Corporation is building the South Island Line (East), the Sha Tin to Central Link and the Kwun Tong Line Extension. In 2018, a new express line is scheduled to link West Kowloon to Shenzhen and the Mainland's high-speed rail network.

Many other projects—ranging from garbage incinerators and columbaria to highways and new towns—are being planned throughout the city. Proposals to recreate the Island Eastern Corridor on the west side of Hong Kong Island and to create a series of artificial islands in Hong Kong waters have also been announced. Under Hong Kong's political system, it is difficult for residents to stop these developments, but the projects are usually subject to a public consultation process and the government occasionally takes public opinion into consideration.

Building new infrastructure creates noise, dust and traffic problems. In Hong Kong, projects also uncover the city's past. In March 2000, workers building an overpass in front of Queen Mary Hospital in Pokfulam discovered a 500-pound bomb that was believed to have been dropped by the American military during the Japanese occupation. Bomb disposal experts burned off 96% of the explosive, which had the potential to seriously damage the hospital, before conducting a controlled detonation that produced a 40-meter-high fireball.[17]

In 2014, thousands of artifacts, including a well and part of a building that are believed to date from the 10th century, were unearthed during the construction of the Sha Tin to Central Link.

Landslides

Each year, Hong Kong experiences 300–400 landslides, which are known locally as landslips. The city's hilly terrain, frequent heavy rainstorms and high population density mean that landslides can have a major impact on the safety and operating cost of a home.

Over the years, landslides have caused hundreds of deaths and millions of dollars of damage. On June 18, 1972, a landslide struck the Sau Mau Ping resettlement area in Kowloon, killing 71 people. The same day, 67 people died when a section of Kotewall Road on Hong Kong Island collapsed, destroying a 12-story apartment block and a six-story building.

A variety of techniques are used to stabilize hillsides in Hong Kong, including shotcrete, drainage channels and concrete retaining walls

In 1976, another landslide hit Sau Mau Ping, killing 18 people and injuring 24. The following year, the government established what is now known as the Geotechnical Engineering Office. In the years that followed, the government introduced a slope safety system and invested billions of dollars in monitoring, drainage improvements and slope stabilization measures. However, landslides continue to represent a serious threat.

If a privately owned slope or retaining wall poses—or is likely to pose—a danger, the Buildings Department issues a statutory order that is registered as an encumbrance against the property with the Land Registry. The slope or retaining wall owner is then required to appoint an Authorized Person to work with a geotechnical engineer and a contractor to assess the condition of the slope or retaining wall and make the necessary repairs. When the government is satisfied that the slope or retaining wall is safe, the encumbrance is discharged.[18]

Mold

Hong Kong's climate supports the growth of mold, particularly *Aspergillus, Cladosporium, Penicillium* and *Stachybotrys*.[19] Mold is a common cause of allergic reactions, such as a runny nose and asthma, and it can cause infections like farmer's lung. Some molds, including *Stachybotrys*, are highly toxic and certain species of *Aspergillus* are carcinogenic. Infants, young children, the elderly and people with chronic diseases are particularly susceptible.

For mold to grow, it needs oxygen, temperatures of between 20°C and 25°C (although *Cladosporium* can be found in refrigerators at -6°C), moisture and food. Many household items, including dust, drywall, food, wood and fabrics provide nutrients for mold.

To prevent mold from growing, ensure adequate levels of ventilation and avoid the use of carpets and wallpaper. Remove sources of water and nutrients, vacuum regularly and promptly dispose of any mold-contaminated items. Clean air filters, air-conditioners and dehumidifiers frequently and use extractor fans in bathrooms and kitchens. Diluted household bleach or a solution of hydrogen peroxide, water and boric acid will kill mold. Household paints containing mold-retardant chemicals are also available.

If your home has a major mold infestation, you may need professional help. In severe cases, this can require precautions—such as airlocks, personal protective equipment and decontamination facilities—like those used in asbestos remediation.[20]

Noise pollution

Long-term exposure to environmental noise has been associated with health problems ranging from hearing loss to obesity and increased incidence of Type 2 diabetes.[21] Children, elderly people, the chronically ill and shift workers are worst affected by high noise levels.

Hong Kong is loud—a problem that is compounded by the city's enthusiasm for construction projects, its high population density and urban planning that puts residential, commercial and industrial buildings in close proximity and expressways within meters of apartment complexes.

A 1998 survey by the Environmental Protection Department found that at 17%, noise pollution was the third most cited social concern, after air pollution (36%) and security (18%). Traffic was named the most annoying form of noise by 55% of respondents, followed by construction at 17%.[22]

The Noise Control Ordinance (Cap. 400) addresses noise from domestic places and public premises, such as televisions and dogs; from construction, including pile drivers and road work; from commercial and industrial facilities; and from alarm systems. Aircraft and occupational noise are regulated by separate ordinances.

Noise from domestic places and public premises is restricted from 23:00 until 07:00. There is no fixed decibel level and complaints are handled by the police on a case-by-case basis. The maximum penalty under this section of the ordinance is $10,000.

Construction work using powered equipment is prohibited between 19:00 and 07:00 and on general holidays, including Sundays, unless a valid construction noise permit is in force. The use of pile drivers requires a permit and is allowed from 07:00 to 19:00, except on holidays.

Depending on the location, pile driving may be allowed for three, five or 12 hours per day.

Industrial and commercial noise is managed using noise abatement notices, which require a building's owner or occupier to meet a given noise level by a specified date. The maximum penalty for a first conviction under this section is $100,000, increasing to $200,000 for second and subsequent offenses, plus $20,000 per day.

Building and vehicle alarms must not sound for more than 15 minutes and five minutes, respectively, with violators subject to a $10,000 fine.

Noise can be reduced by adding acoustic insulation, by filling gaps around windows and doors and by installing double- or triple-glazed windows. However, these measures can be expensive and may not fully solve the problem.

Avoiding predictable noise sources—like traffic, factories and aircraft—is easier than trying to quiet a noisy home. Before you buy, visit the dwelling at different times of the day and night and on weekends and weekdays to accurately gauge the background noise level. Noise is often more noticeable during the winter months, when it is not masked by air conditioners. Check with the government, media and transport operators to see if rail lines or other noisy infrastructure projects are planned for the area.

Sporadic noise, such as a neighbor's party or renovation project, can be harder to manage. Construction companies often view noise-related fines as a cost of doing business, because the fines are almost always less than the liquidated damages payable for late completion of a project.[23] Sometimes, there is little you can do except buy a pair of earplugs and wait for the noise to stop.

Nuclear power

There are no nuclear power plants in Hong Kong, but there are seven operating nuclear reactors in neighboring Guangdong. Six of these are in Daya Bay, which is 50 kilometers from Hong Kong. A further seven plants, many of which have more than one reactor, are planned or under construction in Guangdong.[24]

After the 2011 Fukushima disaster in Japan, China froze its nuclear development program and conducted stress tests on its operating reactors. Some changes and improvements were made, the existing reactors were given a clean bill of health and the development freeze was lifted in November 2012.

On April 26 and 27, 2012, the Hong Kong government conducted an exercise to test Hong Kong's ability to handle a nuclear incident and the Daya Bay Contingency Plan, which was updated after Fukushima. Some 5,200 people participated in the drill, including representatives from the Hong Kong, Macau and central governments and the International Atomic Energy Agency. In a July 2012 Legislative Council report, the Security Bureau stated that the exercise "achieved the objectives that it sets out to achieve."

Some activists dismissed the drill as a public relations exercise. In addition, there are lingering concerns about the accurate and timely flow of information and the government's ability to manage evacuations if there was major nuclear incident.

Plumbing and leaks

Water leaks are common, particularly in older buildings, and can be a source of friction between neighbors. The government recommends that leaks be resolved through discussions. If this is unsuccessful, you can contact the joint office operated by the Buildings Department and the Food and Environmental Hygiene Department through the 1823 telephone hotline. If the source of the leak can be identified and it poses a sanitary nuisance, the joint office can issue an abatement order, requiring the owner to repair the leak. Failure to comply with the order can result in a maximum fine of $10,000 and daily fine of $250. The joint office can also apply to the court for a nuisance order, which carries a maximum fine of $25,000 and a daily fine of $450.[25]

If water leaks through one of the building's common areas into your unit, you will have to negotiate with the management committee. This can happen with walls and roofs, and it can be difficult to apportion costs between the owner and the committee. As I discovered in an industrial unit and an office that I owned, it can also be hard to convince the management committee to take action and spend money.

In extreme cases, you can sue. Between 2006 and 2010 there were 40 such suits, in which plaintiffs were compensated for the cost of repairs, damage to their premises, inconvenience, professional fees and loss of rental income.[26]

Policy risk

Several factors shape Hong Kong's policy environment. These factors influence the government's responses to changes in the property market and the tools that the government uses to manage the market.

▲ The Hong Kong government controls the city's land supply and must strike a balance between protecting the interests of existing homeowners and ensuring that affordable housing is available for everyone.

▲ The Hong Kong dollar's peg to the United States dollar means that the city's interest rates are effectively set in Washington. That prevents the Hong Kong government from using interest rates to cool or stimulate the housing market.

▲ Hong Kong's seven million people are packed into 1,095 square kilometers, two-thirds of which is grassland, wetland and forest. Less than 7% of the city's land was used for residential purposes in 2013.[27]

▲ Despite Hong Kong's reputation for laissez-faire policies, in 2013 more than 45% of the population lived in public housing.[28]

▲ As a special administrative region of China, Hong Kong's politics are unique. Functional constituencies in the Legislative Council, the property cartel and the Heung Yee Kuk exercise significant influence over the housing market. The Chinese government is playing an increasingly prominent role in Hong Kong's affairs and will continue to do so in the run-up to 2047.

⏶ Hong Kong's open economy and independent judicial system make it an attractive investment destination for foreigners, particularly wealthy Mainlanders. This makes Hong Kong vulnerable to flows of "hot money," which distort the property market. To minimize the effect of speculators, the Hong Kong government introduced a special stamp duty in 2010 and a buyer's stamp duty in 2012 and increased the ad valorem stamp duty in 2013. Maximum loan-to-value ratios were reduced in February 2015. Despite these measures, home prices continued to rise.

⏶ While livelihood issues remain a top priority, Hong Kong's citizens are increasingly concerned about the quality of their lives. Clean air, conservation and greater participation in government are recurring themes.

Property bubbles

In 1997, Hong Kong's property market experienced a violent correction. The stage was set in 1996 and the first half of 1997 when real estate prices rebounded from an 18-month slump. On July 1, 1997, Hong Kong reverted to Chinese sovereignty. The next day, the Asian financial crisis began. On October 8, in his maiden policy address, Tung Chee-hwa announced that 85,000 homes would be built each year. From their peak in the third quarter of 1997, home prices fell 50% over the next 12 months and remained in the doldrums through 2003, when severe acute respiratory syndrome killed 300 people in the city. By June 2003, 105,000 mortgages were in negative equity.[29]

With the benefit of hindsight, 1997 was a "perfect storm" that combined inflated property prices, political jitters, an international financial crisis and inexperienced leadership. The outbreak of a mysterious, deadly disease depressed prices and sentiment even further.

Circumstances in 2015 are very different from those in 1997, but Hong Kong's home prices are high, interest rates are set to rise and an ascendant China is testing its economic and political might. Any combination of these factors—or a black swan event—could cause a drop in Hong Kong's property prices.

Public housing

In Hong Kong, about 3.5 million people live in subsidized housing, including rented and owned apartments, and more than 240,000 people are on public housing waiting lists.[30] Over 200 public housing estates, most of which are provided by the Hong Kong Housing Authority, are distributed throughout the city. Some estates are 50 years old, while others are new.

There is a stigma associated with living in public housing. Unemployment, mental illness and criminal activity, including drugs, smuggling and gambling, are not uncommon. That said, Hong Kong's public housing estates are generally safe, clean and pleasant.

Through the Home Ownership Scheme, the government helps people who earn too much to qualify for public rental housing but not enough to buy an apartment from a private developer. Apartments purchased through this program can be sold, with restrictions, on the secondary market.

Nearly half of Hong Kong's population lives in public housing estates, like this one in Tin Shui Wai.

In cities such as London and New York, new private complexes often have a public component, which the developer builds in exchange for planning approval, additional floor area or similar concessions. In Hong Kong, public housing complexes are separate from private blocks, although private dwellings may be found in the area. For investors, abundant public housing can depress the prices and rents of nearby private homes.

Radon

Radon is a colorless, odorless, tasteless, radioactive gas that occurs from the natural decay of uranium in soil and rocks, particularly granite. When radon breaks down, it produces decay products that cause lung cancer. A 1988 study estimated that radon was associated with 13% of the lung cancer deaths in Hong Kong. Like asbestos, radon poses a greater hazard to smokers than nonsmokers.[31]

Radon risk is usually associated with basements because radon rises from the earth and enters buildings through cracks and holes in their foundations. In Hong Kong, however, most people live in high-rise apartments that are built from concrete containing granite. As a result, radon is present throughout the building, although concentrations tend to be reduced on higher floors. Commercial buildings that are sealed to save energy or where the ventilation system has not been properly maintained often have radon levels that are higher than those in residential buildings.

Maintaining adequate airflow, either through open windows or a mechanical ventilation system, reduces radon risk in high-rise buildings. Radon barriers, such as wallpaper, tile and paint, reduce indoor radon concentrations by 20%–80%.[32]

Schools

The primary grades of Hong Kong's international schools will have a shortage of more than 4,000 places in the 2016/17 academic year.[33] The lack of space is less of a problem for secondary students because older children often attend boarding school abroad.

Local chambers of commerce say the shortage hinders the expansion of businesses in Hong Kong. It's also making young children endure hour-long bus rides to schools in distant parts of the city each day.

Sick building syndrome

Sick building syndrome (SBS) is a group of nonspecific symptoms that includes headaches; coughing; irritation of the eyes, nose, throat or skin; dizziness; nausea; difficulty concentrating; and fatigue. There is no standard clinical definition for SBS, but people suffering from this condition usually feel better shortly after they leave the building.

A definitive cause for SBS has not been identified, but it is associated with indoor air pollution, particularly from the volatile organic compounds (VOCs) in adhesives, furniture, wall coverings, paint, flooring, wood products, solvents and cleaning solutions, pesticides and other products. Polluted outdoor air that is drawn into a building can also contribute to SBS.

Because VOCs are used in construction materials, SBS is common in new and newly renovated homes, especially dwellings that have been sealed to increase their energy efficiency. SBS has also been linked to biological contaminants such as mold, bacteria, viruses and pollen and is exacerbated by inadequate ventilation and poor building maintenance.

Children are more susceptible to SBS and other forms of environmental chemical exposure than adults. Homemakers and other people who spend a great deal of time at home are also at risk. Psychosocial factors such as stress and anxiety can play a role in SBS, and some researchers have questioned whether SBS (and related conditions such as multiple chemical sensitivity and idiopathic environmental intolerance) is a panic attack triggered by exposure to "chemical" smells.

Airborne chemicals can be removed via physisorption with activated charcoal, porous ceramics and natural fibers; by chemisorption using organic and inorganic compounds; and through decomposition using photocatalysts, negative ions and other techniques. Commercial products, such as electronic air cleaners and passive air cleaning boards that use manganese dioxide to convert formaldehyde into water and carbon dioxide, are also available, as are colorimetric detectors that indicate the presence of formaldehyde. Increasing the flow of outside air can also help.

A 2009 survey of indoor environmental quality found that nasal dis-
comfort, including sneezing and a runny nose, was the most common
home-related SBS symptom. Based on data from 748 households in
Hong Kong's Yau Tsim Mong District, the finding was noteworthy
because the homes did not have central ventilation systems, which,
along with sealed buildings, are often associated with SBS.[34] The same
study showed that 58% of respondents were dissatisfied with noise
from inside the building, versus 17% who were unhappy with outside
noise and 17% who were dissatisfied with their building's ventilation.

Soil pollution

Contaminated soil is often found on brownfield sites, which are old
industrial facilities like factories, refineries, garages and warehouses.
Contaminants include heavy metals, such as arsenic, cadmium, chro-
mium, lead and mercury; electronic waste, such as flame retardants;
organic chemicals like hydrocarbons and solvents; and persistent
organic pollutants, including polychlorinated biphenyls (PCBs) and
pesticides like DDT. Exposure to these substances can cause cancer
and other diseases.

In Hong Kong, soil pollution comes from many sources. For example,
while the sale of leaded gasoline was banned in 1999, lead from vehicle emissions is still found in urban soils.[35]

Old neighborhoods like North Point, industrial areas such as Kwun
Tong and districts with busy roads have elevated heavy metal levels. On Hong Kong Island, the Sheung Wan–Causeway Bay corridor,
Taikoo Shing, Shau Kei Wan, Aberdeen and Wong Chuk Hang are hot
spots. Levels of heavy metals are generally higher in soil samples tak-
en from urban areas than from suburban or rural locations.[36]

The New Territories poses a special challenge. Hong Kong's farmland
has dropped from more than 13,000 hectares in the 1970s to less than
6,000 hectares in 2010. Large amounts of agricultural land are now
used for car dismantling operations and for electronic waste recycling,
including dismantling and open burning workshops.[37] A 2010 study
of six e-waste processing sites in the New Territories found levels of
heavy metals and persistent organic pollutants exceeded Canadian,
Chinese and Dutch standards by three to 46 times.[38] A 2013 study of

five car dismantling workshops found similar levels of contamination from polycyclic aromatic hydrocarbons and other chemicals.

Most Hong Kong residents live in apartments, where they have little direct contact with soil. However, soil pollution can leach into the groundwater, enter the food chain and become household dust, which is inhaled by residents and ingested by children. Research by Susanna Tong and Kin Che Lam suggests that dust containing heavy metals enters Hong Kong homes through open windows and is tracked in from balconies. Removing carpets from floors, closing windows and vacuuming and sweeping regularly help to alleviate dust-related heavy metal pollution.[39]

Hong Kong's Center for Health Protection notes that lead paint, cosmetics and herbal medicines can produce hazardous levels of non-occupational lead exposure, while contaminated food and urban dust can result in very low level exposure.

Statutory orders, notices and directions

Under the Buildings Ordinance (Cap. 123), the Buildings Department issues statutory orders for unauthorized building works (S. 24); the investigation of buildings (S. 26A); repairs to buildings (S. 26); dangerous hillsides (S. 27A); the investigation and repair of water pipes, drains or sewers in slopes (S. 27); and drainage repairs (S. 28).

Statutory orders (SOs) require the building owner to take a specific action, such as demolishing an unauthorized structure or repairing a broken drain, within a fixed time. If the owner fails to comply, he can be fined or jailed. If necessary, the Buildings Department can take corrective action, such as stabilizing a dangerous hillside, and recover the cost from the owners. SOs may be appealed to the Building Appeal Tribunal.

An SO is registered as an encumbrance against the property in the Land Registry, where it remains until the corrective action is taken. An outstanding SO can reduce the value of a property, making it hard to sell. If you buy a property with an outstanding SO, you may have difficulty arranging a mortgage. When an SO is issued for a problem involving a building's common area, the encumbrance affects the title of all units in the building until the corrective action is taken and the SO is discharged.[40]

Notices and directions can also be issued by other government departments. The Water Supplies Department issues notices under the Waterworks Ordinance (Cap. 102) if waterworks are altered without proper authorization or the supplied water is wasted or polluted. The Environmental Protection Department issues notices under the Water Pollution Control Ordinance (Cap. 358) for drainage systems that are not properly connected to the public sewage system. The Fire Services Department issues fire hazard abatement notices under the Fire Services Ordinance (Cap. 95).

The Electrical and Mechanical Services Department issues notices under the Electricity Ordinance (Cap. 406) for repairs, maintenance and testing of a building's wiring; under the Gas Safety Ordinance (Cap. 51) for repairs, maintenance and testing of the building's gas system; and under the Lift and Escalator (Safety) Ordinance (Cap. 327) for elevators that do not comply with regulations.

The Food and Environmental Hygiene Department issues notices under the Public Health and Municipal Services Ordinance (Cap. 132) for repairs to drain pipes and cleaning private sewers.

Subsidence

Subsidence is a drop or depression in the earth's surface that is often caused by groundwater depletion and underground construction. In Hong Kong, reclaimed land is prone to subsidence.

Subsidence can create large bills for homeowners, who must repair and reinforce foundations. In extreme cases, it can leave a building uninhabitable. Subsidence can also damage sewers, as well as water, gas and electricity supplies.

Several areas in the New Territories have been affected by subsidence. In Tin Shui Wai, four towers in Tin Fu Court, a public housing estate, experienced foundation problems and cracked walls.[41] In Tsueng Kwan O, buildings in three public housing estates—Tong Ming Court, Sheung Tak Estate and Beverly Garden—developed cracks in their walls, ceilings and floors that were believed to be caused by subsidence.[42] On Ning Garden, which is also in Tseung Kwan O, experienced similar problems.

In addition to Tseung Kwan O, where land was reclaimed in the 1980s, subsidence has been reported in Kwai Chung. Residents have also expressed concerns that work on the express rail line linking West Kowloon with Shenzhen might result in subsidence and damage buildings in Tai Kok Tsui.

Termites

Termites are an important part of the global ecosystem, helping to break down plant matter and aerate soil. There are more than 2,600 species of termites, about 10% of which are considered pests.

More than 10 species have been identified in Hong Kong, including *Cryptotermes brevis, Reticulitermes fukienensis, Capritermes fuscotibialis, Procapritermes sowerbyi, Macrotermes barneyi* and *Odontotermes formosanus.* The Formosan subterranean termite, *Coptotermes formosanus,* is the most common termite in Hong Kong.[43]

Known in Hong Kong as white ants, termites consume cupboards, door frames, paper, wooden floors and similar materials. They can also destroy plaster, PVC pipe, electric cables and other soft materials.[44]

Termite damage can be difficult to detect until it has reached an advanced stage, so a professional inspection is wise if you suspect your home is infested. The presence of shelter tubes, which termites use as protection from the elements and predators, frass (termite excrement) and shed wings are indications of a problem. Infested homes are usually treated by killing the colony with insecticides or chemicals and then introducing barriers to prevent the termites from returning.

Unauthorized building works

Unauthorized building works (UBWs) are alterations or additions to the inside or outside of a structure that are made without the Buildings Department's approval. This includes new structures, such as a sun room added to a village house, major alternations, such as subdividing an apartment, and seemingly innocuous changes, like adding a canopy or enclosing a balcony.

The government takes a tough stand on UBWs, particularly those posing a health, safety or environmental hazard. UBWs are discovered by Buildings Department inspectors, by contractors hired by the department and by reports to a telephone hotline. When a UBW is found, the Buildings Department issues a statutory order, which is registered as an encumbrance with the Land Registry. Owners who fail to comply with a statutory order can be jailed for one year and fined $200,000 plus $20,000 per day that the offense continues.[45]

Many UBWs have existed for years, but this does not make them legal. Paying rates on an illegal structure does not make the structure legal, and the Buildings Department can demand the removal of an otherwise legal and structurally sound addition because the owner did not receive approval before construction. The department can also require that an alteration, like new balustrades on a balcony, be returned to its original condition, at which point the owner can apply for permission to return the balcony to its improved state.

Not all UBWs have been cataloged and buyers can be forced to pay for the demolition and reconstruction of parts of their newly purchased home. In addition to being expensive to fix, UBWs can affect a home's safety, especially if load-bearing walls or emergency exits have been improperly modified.

UBWs can be political. Leung Chun-ying, Hong Kong's third chief executive, and his rival for the post, Henry Tang, were both found to have illegal structures in their homes in 2012. Meanwhile, a 2012 crackdown on an estimated 200,000 UBWs in the New Territories resulted in protests but little enforcement action.[46]

Consult an engineer, surveyor or architect if you suspect that a property you plan to buy has a UBW. The Buildings Department offers an online service called BRAVO and a walk-in service at the Building Information Center in Mongkok where you can view and request copies of building plans and related documents. Both services exclude prewar buildings, exempted houses in the New Territories and former Housing Authority buildings.

Water

About 20%–30% of Hong Kong's drinking water comes from local catchments, with the balance from Guangdong's Dongjiang (East River) via a dedicated aqueduct. Water pollution is a serious problem in China and the Hong Kong government works with the Guangdong authorities to improve and protect the quality of the water that Hong Kong imports.

Hong Kong's water quality meets the standards set by the World Health Organization. The city has 21 facilities where drinking water is filtered and treated with chlorine, fluoride and other chemicals. The Water Supplies Department publishes a biological and chemical analysis of the water it receives from Guangdong as well as the water it supplies to consumers in Hong Kong.

Freshwater and the seawater used to flush toilets in most parts of the city are delivered through a 7,800-kilometer network of water mains, most of which are buried. The Water Supplies Department is responsible for the water mains up to a building or lot's boundaries. The incorporated owners are responsible for the water mains and associated facilities in the streets and communal areas of private housing estates. Individual consumers are responsible for the internal plumbing serving their apartments.

In July 2015, lead levels exceeding WHO standards were found in drinking water samples taken from Kai Ching Estate, a public housing complex in Kowloon. In the weeks that followed, lead was discovered in water at 10 more public housing estates, two primary schools and at least one private sector estate, The Caldecott in Kowloon. In some cases, the lead was more than 21 times the safe level.

The Hong Kong government appointed a commission of inquiry, which is scheduled to report to Hong Kong's chief executive by March 2016. In the meantime, many owners' corporations arranged private tests of their water supplies.

Wildlife

Hong Kong is home to a variety of wildlife, including Burmese pythons, monkeys, wild pigs and water buffalo. You are more likely to encounter these creatures in the New Territories, but snakes and wild pigs are also seen on Hong Kong Island. Rats are common throughout the city.

Feral cattle and water buffalo are a common sight on Lantau's Cheung Sha Beach.

HONG KONG'S
HOUSING MARKET

Demographics

Where to Live

DEMOGRAPHICS

Demographic trends—including aging, declining fertility, immigration and emigration—shape Hong Kong's real estate market. The city is also influenced by political decisions that are made in China and by the activities of Mainland mothers, shoppers and investors.

Population snapshot

Hong Kong's Census and Statistics Department conducts a census every five years. In 2011, Hong Kong's population was 7.7 million, up from 6.9 million in 2006.

There were 876 men for every 1,000 women (2006: 912), and the population had a median age of 41.7 years (2006: 39.6).

Children aged 0–14 years accounted for 11.6% of the population (2006: 13.7%), adults aged 15–64 were 75.1% (2006: 73.9%) and people over 65 represented 13.3% (2006: 12.4%).

The life expectancy at birth was 80.3 years for men (2006: 79.4) and 86.7 for women (2006: 85.5). The total fertility rate, defined as the number of live births for every 1,000 women, was 1,204 (2006: 984).

The crude marriage rate per 1,000 people was 8.2 (2006: 7.3), and the crude divorce rate per 1,000 people was 2.8 (2006: 2.5).[1]

Nearly 94% of Hong Kong people are of Chinese ethnicity, with other Asians comprising just over 5%. Whites, people of mixed race and others each represent less than 1%.[2] More than 300,000 people, mainly women from Indonesia and the Philippines, are employed as domestic helpers.

Hong Kong had 2.4 million households (2006: 2.3 million) with an average size of 2.9 persons (2006: 3.0).

Hong Kong is one of the most densely populated places on earth. In mid-2014 the land population was 6,690 people per square kilometer.

Kwun Tong, which had 57,250 people per square kilometer, is the city's most densely populated district.[3]

Hong Kong's population

Aging
Like many developed economies, Hong Kong has an aging population. By 2026, nearly one-quarter of Hong Kong's people will be over 65. That proportion will rise to almost one-third by 2041, when the median age will reach 51.8.[4]

As the population ages, the city's dependency ratio will fall from 5.3 working-aged people (i.e., those aged 15–64) for each retiree in 2011 to 1.8:1 in 2041. The total labor force is expected to peak in 2018 and then decline until it begins to stabilize in 2030.

In 2013, one-third of the elderly population lived below the poverty line.[5] The government is under pressure to supplement the modest level of financial aid provided through the Comprehensive Social Security Assistance and Old Age Living Allowance programs, as well as the Mandatory Provident Fund scheme, a compulsory retirement savings plan that was introduced in 2000. Spending on public health care will also increase to meet the needs of an aging population.

The combination of fewer people paying salaries tax and increased social welfare spending could result in higher tax rates, including property-related taxes. In addition, Hong Kong will need workers to care for the elderly, an area where foreign domestic helpers now play an important role.

Marriage
Fewer Hong Kong women are getting married. In 1991, 54% of women aged 25–29 were married. By 2011, that number had dropped to 27%. Women are also marrying later, with the median age at first marriage rising from 26.2 in 1991 to 28.9 in 2011.

Rapidly aging population

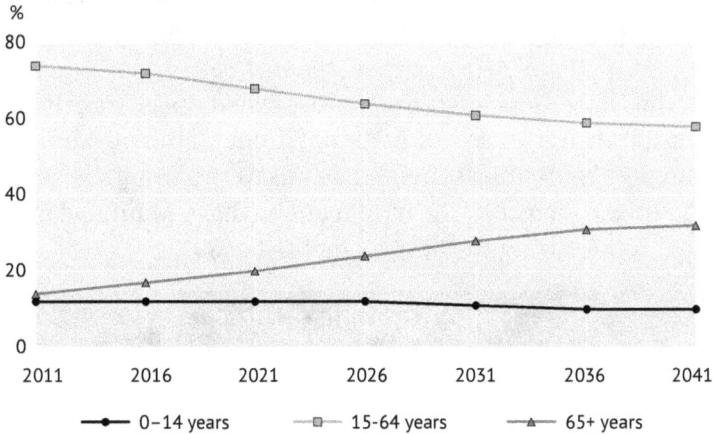

When Hong Kong people marry, many pick a partner from the Mainland. In 2013, 21,030 marriages, or 38% of the total, were between a Hong Kong resident and a person from the Mainland. The number of Hong Kong men marrying Mainland brides slipped from 21,220 in 1991 to 19,166 in 2013. But local women marrying Mainland men rose more than fivefold, from 1,390 in 1991 to 7,444 in 2013. Unlike Hong Kong, the Mainland has a surplus of men.

Divorce is becoming more common, with the crude divorce rate per 1,000 people increasing from 1.1 in 1991 to 2.8 in 2011.

More Hong Kong women are choosing to remain single. In the 40–44 age group, the percentage of women who have never married jumped from 6% in 1991 to 17% in 2011.

Children
Hong Kong women are having fewer babies. The number of births dropped steadily from 86,751 in 1981 to 46,965 in 2003 before rebounding to 95,451 in 2011.

However, the rebound is deceptive. In 2011, nearly 44,000 of Hong Kong's newborns had Mainland mothers. In addition to the high quality of its hospitals, Hong Kong is an attractive place for Mainland women to give birth because of a 2001 ruling by Hong Kong's Court of Final Appeal that Chinese citizens born in the city are Hong Kong permanent residents regardless of their parents' immigration status.

In 2013, the Hong Kong government instructed the city's private and public hospitals not to accept bookings from Mainland women who wished to give birth unless their husbands were permanent residents of Hong Kong. As a result, the number of births to Mainland mothers fell to just 3,183 during the first six months of 2013.[6]

Hong Kong birth rates

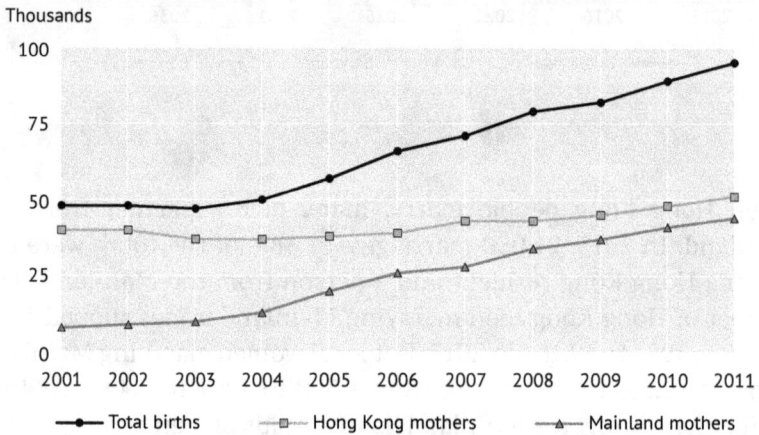

Thousands

Total births   Hong Kong mothers   Mainland mothers

Emigration

Hong Kong people have a long history of emigration. Tens of thousands of people departed after the leftist riots that began in May 1967. Over six months, 51 people were killed, 800 were injured in riots, 300 were wounded by bombs and more than 5,000 were jailed.[7]

Another wave of emigration began after China and the United Kingdom signed the Joint Declaration—which set the stage for Hong Kong's return to China—in December 1984. Sixty-thousand people left Hong Kong between 1984 and 1986, with almost 30,000 emigrating in 1987 alone.

In 1990, the year after the Tiananmen Square massacre, 65,000 emigrated. Between 1984 and 1997, Hong Kong lost about 10% of its population. These were educated, bilingual entrepreneurs and professionals who were desirable new citizens for Canada, Australia, New Zealand, the United States and other countries.

As the worst-case scenarios failed to materialize after the city's return to China, many emigres returned to Hong Kong with second passports. One estimate claimed that in 2013, there were more than 350,000 Canadian passport holders in Hong Kong.[8] If the political climate in Hong Kong were to deteriorate, these people could depart for Canada, destabilizing the city's property market.

Some commentators have suggested that the discontent behind the Occupy Central protests in 2014 could spark a new wave of emigration. There is no data to support this assertion, but Hong Kong people are mobile and have an international outlook.

In addition, the Hong Kong government estimated that in 2011 about 110,000 Hong Kong retirees had moved to the Mainland. However, rising inflation, a stronger yuan and difficulty accessing health care make China a less attractive retirement destination for Hong Kong people.[9]

Distribution projections
In 2013, Hong Kong's Planning Department estimated that, by mid-2021:

▲ The population of the New Territories will increase 10.4%, to 4.1 million, and represent more than 53% of Hong Kong's total.

▲ Nearly half of Hong Kong's new residents will live in new towns in the New Territories. Tuen Mun will account for almost 7% of Hong Kong's population. The proportion of people aged over 65 in new towns will reach 17.2%, up from 10.9% in 2011.

▲ Wanchai will be the district with the highest proportion of over-65s, with the gray population swelling to 23.8%, from 15.6% in 2011. Sai Kung will have the highest share of residents aged 15–64, although this figure will fall to 74.5%, from 78.1% in 2011. Yau Tsim

Mong will have the highest proportion of children aged 0–14, rising
to 15.5%, from 12.3% in 2011.[10]

China's influence

Immigrants

As John Carroll notes in *A Concise History of Hong Kong*, the city has
long served as a haven for Mainland refugees. Exiles arrived during
the Taiping Rebellion (1851–64), the Republican Revolution in 1911,
throughout the 1920s, after the outbreak of the Sino-Japanese War in
1937 and following the Communist Revolution in 1949. From 1974 to
1980, Hong Kong's Touch Base Policy allowed illegal immigrants to
stay if they evaded immigration officials and reached the city's urban
areas.

Today, Mainland people arrive in a variety of ways. For instance, between 2001 and 2013, more than 304,000 babies were born in Hong
Kong to Mainland mothers. The majority of these babies are believed
to have returned to the Mainland, but they have the right to settle in
Hong Kong at a later date.

Mainland spouses and accompanying children of Hong Kong residents can apply to move to Hong Kong through the One-Way Permit
Scheme, which is run by the central government. With a quota of 150
migrants per day, nearly half a million people—mainly women and
children—used this program between 2003 and mid-2013.

The Hong Kong government introduced the Admission Scheme for
Mainland Talents and Professionals in 2003. By the end of 2013, more
than 65,000 Mainlanders had arrived through this program.[11]

Hong Kong almost had another 1.7 million residents, who the Hong
Kong government estimated would cost $170 billion to house and ed-
ucate. In January 1999, the Court of Final Appeal ruled that—under
Article 24 of the Basic Law—children acquire right of abode (also
known as permanent residency) in Hong Kong if, at or after the time of
their birth, at least one parent was a Hong Kong permanent resident.
Later that year, the Standing Committee of the National People's
Congress issued an interpretation of the Basic Law stating that for a

child to obtain right of abode in Hong Kong, one or more parents must be a Hong Kong permanent resident at the time of the child's birth.[12]

Home buyers
Mainland citizens buy homes in Hong Kong for many reasons, including the city's deep, liquid property market and its lack of capital controls and restrictions on the number of properties that a person can own. They are also attracted by the ability to buy using a company.

Tracking the number of Mainland buyers and their impact on the market is difficult, because the Hong Kong government does not record the origin of nonlocal buyers. To gather this information, researchers count the number of buyers with Putonghua names. However, this method overstates the number of Mainland buyers because it includes people from the Mainland who have become permanent residents of Hong Kong.

Mainland buyers are believed to represent between 10% and 35% of new home purchases, with the proportion varying with the economic climate. The number of Mainland buyers has fallen as a result of the buyer's stamp duty that was introduced in 2012.

Shoppers
Mainland people shop in Hong Kong because of the city's low taxes. In addition, some brands and products are available in Hong Kong, but not in China's secondary and tertiary cities. Shoppers are also confident that products sold in Hong Kong are of high quality and that branded goods, such as Louis Vuitton bags, are not counterfeit.

The rise of Mainland shoppers is relatively new and has been driven by higher disposable incomes in China and the introduction of the Individual Visit Scheme (IVS), which now allows people from 49 cities to visit Hong Kong without an escort. Launched in July 2003, the scheme was a joint effort by the central and Hong Kong governments to boost the city's economy, which was suffering from the effects of the severe acute respiratory syndrome outbreak. In 2013, Hong Kong received 40.7 million visitors from the Mainland, more than two-thirds of whom were traveling under the IVS.

In 2009, Shenzhen residents were allowed to apply for multiple-entry permits under the IVS. The new visas facilitated the activities of parallel traders, who would buy products in Hong Kong for resale on the Mainland. Some traders made several trips to Hong Kong each day, resulting in product shortages, laws limiting exports of baby formula and public protests. Parallel traders were also blamed for rising prices, as stores selling daily necessities in places like Sheung Shui, Fanling and Sha Tin were displaced by outlets catering to Mainland tourists. According to the Hong Kong government, between 2004 and 2013, the number of stores selling cosmetics and personal care items rose 1,500% and shop rents increased 69.4%.[13] In April 2015, after violent scuffles between locals and Mainland shoppers, Shenzhen residents were restricted to one trip per week.

The influence of Mainland shoppers is not limited to locations near the boundary. Rents for retail space, as well as the mix of stores in neighborhoods and shopping malls throughout Hong Kong are affected by Mainland tourists' tastes and demands. As the quality of China's stores improves, distribution and logistics become more efficient, tariffs on imported products are cut and anti-piracy efforts become more effective, Hong Kong will be a less compelling destination for Mainland shoppers. That, in turn, could cause a drop in the price of commercial property in Hong Kong.

WHERE TO LIVE

Here is an overview of popular residential areas in Hong Kong. Figures quoted are asking prices, as of August 2015.

Discovery Bay

Located on Lantau Island, Discovery Bay (www.dbay.hk) is a 649-hectare integrated development built and operated by Hong Kong Resort Company. The development's 18,000 residents enjoy convenient access to Hong Kong International Airport and Hong Kong Disneyland.

Selection
Discovery Bay includes garden homes, as well as low-, mid- and high-rise apartments. A 400-square-foot apartment costs $3.5 million, while 4,800-square-foot houses start at $100 million.

Amenities
Discovery Bay has international, primary and preschools, residents' clubs, a golf club, a marina, medical clinics, shopping and restaurants.

Transport
Discovery Bay is linked to Hong Kong Island by a 24-hour ferry service, which berths in Central. Ferry service is also available to Mui Wo and Peng Chau. Hong Kong Resort operates a bus service inside Discovery Bay. A tunnel links Discovery Bay to the North Lantau Expressway and there are bus services to Sunny Bay, Tung Chung and Hong Kong International Airport. Private cars are banned in Discovery Bay.

Advantages
Discovery Bay offers good value for money. As a planned community, it is more orderly and less chaotic than other parts of Hong Kong. Some expatriates, who comprise about half the population, appreciate Discovery Bay's calm environment.

Drawbacks
Many people who work on Hong Kong Island rely on the ferry service, which can be disrupted during typhoons. Disputes about facilities

and services have occurred between residents and Hong Kong Resort, which runs the development. Some people find Discovery Bay sterile.

Happy Valley, Tai Hang and Jardine's Lookout

Located near the center of Hong Kong Island, Happy Valley, Tai Hang and Jardine's Lookout are close to the city's business district. Many high-rises have views of Victoria Harbor or the Hong Kong Jockey Club's Happy Valley Racecourse.

Selection
These neighborhoods offer a diverse range of dwellings that include multiple high-rise towers, like Cavendish Heights in Jardine's Lookout, mid-rise buildings in Happy Valley and older walk-ups in Tai Hang. Prices start at $4 million for a Happy Valley studio apartment, with houses in Jardine's Lookout costing over $200 million.

Amenities
The area has a good selection of schools, including the French and Japanese international schools. The privately operated Adventist Hospital and the Hong Kong Sanatorium & Hospital are nearby, as is Causeway Bay, one of Hong Kong's most popular shopping destinations. Happy Valley has a good selection of restaurants and bistros.

Transport
Happy Valley is served by a tram line, and Happy Valley and Tai Hang are within walking distance of Mass Transit Railway (MTR) stations in Causeway Bay and Tin Hau, respectively. The area is well served by buses and minibuses.

Advantages
Happy Valley, Tai Hang and Jardine's Lookout are convenient to the offices and shops on the east side of Hong Kong Island. Jardine's Lookout has large apartments as well as a selection of houses. Happy Valley is an older neighborhood with a village ambience.

Drawbacks
Traffic on race days at the Happy Valley Racecourse can be heavy. During the Rugby Sevens, which is held at Hong Kong Stadium every spring, the area can be chaotic.

The islands

Hong Kong's inhabited outlying islands include Cheung Chau, Lamma, Lantau, Peng Chau and Tsing Yi. In addition to Discovery Bay, Lantau has several residential areas, including Mui Wo, Ma Wan, Pui O, Sea Ranch and Tung Chung, a modern development adjacent to Hong Kong International Airport.

Selection
For the most part, homes on the islands are multi-tower complexes like those found in Tung Chung, Tsing Yi and the Park Island development in Ma Wan, or village houses, some of which include a rooftop patio and garden. Prices range from $3 million for a one-bedroom apartment in Mui Wo to $30 million for a 1,600-square-foot, four-bedroom apartment in Tung Chung.

Amenities
Amenities vary widely. Tsing Yi, Ma Wan and Tung Chung are modern developments with services and infrastructure to match. Rural villages offer basic shopping and restaurants and bars, but you will have to travel to Kowloon or Hong Kong Island for specialty items. The beachfront Sea Ranch has no amenities, so residents must shop on Cheung Chau.

Transport
Tsing Yi is a transport hub that is served by several highways and the MTR's Airport Express and Tung Chung lines. The Tung Chung Line links Tung Chung to Central, and Tung Chung, Tsing Yi and Ma Wan have bus services. Tung Chung and Ma Wan have ferry services, while Lamma, Cheung Chau, Peng Chau and Sea Ranch are only accessible by ferry. A ferry service connects Mui Wo to Central, and Mui Wo has bus services to Tung Chung and other destinations.

Advantages
The islands offer good value for money. Tung Chung and Tsing Yi are convenient for people who fly frequently or work at the airport. Island villages can be relaxed and quiet with a green environment.

Drawbacks
Long commutes and ferry schedules can constrain your lifestyle. Older children often attend schools on Hong Kong Island or in Kowloon. Village politics can be annoying and the islands are swamped by day-trippers on weekends and holidays. Wildlife, such as snakes and water buffalo, are common in rural areas.

Some outlying islands, like Cheung Chau, are only accessible by ferry.

Kowloon Tong

Located in the north-central part of the Kowloon Peninsula, Kowloon Tong is the most exclusive district in Kowloon. An old, established neighborhood with broad, shady streets, Kowloon Tong is popular with wealthy businesspeople and entertainers.

Selection
Detached and semidetached houses and low-rise apartment buildings make up most of the accommodations in Kowloon Tong. Two-bedroom apartments start at $7 million, while houses sell for $200 million–$300 million.

Amenities
Kowloon Tong has excellent amenities, including several international schools, Hong Kong Baptist University and City University of Hong Kong. Festival Walk—a large, modern shopping mall—is nearby and there are several parks in the neighborhood.

Transport
Kowloon Tong Station is an interchange for the MTR's Kwun Tong and East Rail lines. Route 1, which leads to Sha Tin and Tsim Sha Tsui, is nearby.

Advantages
This is the preferred neighborhood for low-rise living in Kowloon. It is mature and pleasant and has excellent services and facilities. Kowloon Tong is convenient for people who travel frequently to China.

Drawbacks
Kowloon Tong is expensive. People who work on Hong Kong Island spend a fair amount of time in the Cross-Harbor Tunnel.

Mid-Levels

With the Peak above and the Sheung Wan–Causeway Bay corridor below, Mid-Levels encompasses a range of neighborhoods and styles. Many apartments have harbor views, clubhouses and shuttle buses.

Selection
In Mid-Levels, apartments are the norm. There are some colonial-era, low-rise buildings on Kennedy Road and MacDonnell Road and high-rise buildings on Conduit, Robinson and Caine roads. Homes range from 300-square-foot studios, which start at $4.5 million, to 7,000-square-foot penthouses that cost hundreds of millions of dollars.

Amenities
Mid-Levels is well served by hospitals, schools, restaurants and shops, many of which are within walking distance of Bonham, Caine, Conduit and Robinson roads. SoHo is home to many popular restaurants and bars, and the Lan Kwai Fong entertainment area is nearby.

The Hong Kong Zoological and Botanical Gardens and Hong Kong Park are also in Mid-Levels.

Transport
The Central–Mid-Levels Escalator, which runs downhill in the morning and uphill in the afternoon and evening, connects Conduit, Robinson, Caine and Hollywood roads with Central. Taxis, buses and minibuses are plentiful in Mid-Levels and the MTR's Central and Hong Kong stations are a short distance away.

Advantages
Residents of Mid-Levels can walk to Central. The area has good access to services and is less expensive than the Peak.

Drawbacks
Mid-Levels' high population density can be claustrophobic. The main thoroughfares—Bonham, Caine, Conduit, Hollywood, Kennedy, MacDonnell and Robinson roads—have only two lanes, so rush-hour traffic jams are common.

The Peak

Hong Kong's most prestigious—and most expensive—properties are on the Peak, which is situated at the very top of Hong Kong Island. The Peak offers spectacular views of Victoria Harbor and the south side of Hong Kong Island and is popular with top-level executives.

Selection
Low-rise apartments, as well as detached and semidetached houses are available on the Peak. You can pay hundreds of millions of dollars for a house, with apartments starting at $35 million.

Amenities
Matilda International Hospital, a private facility, is located on the Peak. The Peak Galleria offers restaurants, supermarkets and other shops, although many outlets cater to tourists. The English Schools Foundation operates Peak School for primary students. The German Swiss International School is also located on the Peak.

Transport
The Peak Tram, a funicular railway, links the Peak to Mid-Levels and Central. The Peak is well served by taxis, buses and minibuses, although most residents either drive or have drivers.

Advantages
Nothing says you have arrived like an address on the Peak. The Peak's cool breezes are a welcome relief during Hong Kong's hot summers, and the Peak offers a good selection of colonial-era apartments with high ceilings and generous proportions.

Drawbacks
The Peak is often cloaked in clouds, obscuring the view and causing condensation and mold inside homes. The commute to Central is not particularly convenient. Tour buses can be a nuisance.

Matilda Hospital on the Peak is one of Hong Kong's oldest hospitals.

Pokfulam

Located on the west side of Hong Kong Island, Pokfulam is known for its schools and green hillsides. Recently completed developments include The Belcher's and Bel-Air. Many Pokfulam apartments offer sunny, western exposure and views of the Lamma Channel.

Selection

Accommodations in Pokfulam are mainly low- and mid-rise apartments, with a selection of houses available in Bel-Air. Apartments in Pokfulam range from 300-square-foot studios, which sell for about $5 million, to 3,000-square-foot homes at about $100 million. Developments such as Scenic Villas and Baguio Villas are more than 30 years old and offer high ceilings and high efficiency ratios.

Amenities

The government-run Queen Mary Hospital is in Pokfulam, as is the University of Hong Kong, primary and secondary schools operated by the English Schools Foundation and the privately run Kellett School. Shopping, dining and entertainment options have improved with the opening of the Cyberport complex.

Pokfulam is noted for its schools and for a cemetery that is run by the Hong Kong Chinese Christian Churches Union.

Transport

Pokfulam is well served by taxis, buses and minibuses. An extension to the MTR's South Island Line, with stations at the University of Hong Kong, Cyberport, Wah Fu, Aberdeen and Wong Chuk Hang, is in the planning stages. An extension to the MTR's Island Line, with a stop in nearby Kennedy Town, opened at the end of 2014.

Advantages

Pokfulam offers a quieter, greener environment than Mid-Levels and good value for money. West Kowloon and the International Commerce Center are easily accessible via buses using the Western Harbor Tunnel.

Drawbacks

You will probably need a car or public transit for shopping and dining out. Many people think Pokfulam is far from Central, although this is more perception than reality. The Hong Kong Chinese Christian Churches Union Pokfulam Road Cemetery limits the area's attractiveness to some buyers.

Sai Kung and Clear Water Bay

Located in the eastern New Territories, Sai Kung and Clear Water Bay offer a relaxed lifestyle and good air quality. Nearby marinas, beaches and country parks make these districts popular with people who enjoy outdoor activities.

Selection

Most of the homes in Sai Kung and Clear Water Bay are low-rise apartments, detached and semidetached houses and village houses. Many houses have sea views, gardens and swimming pools. In Sai Kung, 300-square-foot studio apartments cost less than $2 million. Houses on generous lots are $200 million–$300 million.

Amenities

Sai Kung offers a growing number of pubs and restaurants, particularly ones specializing in seafood. Basic shopping is available in Sai Kung and Clear Water Bay. Tseung Kwan O is the nearest major center. The English Schools Foundation operates a primary school in Clear Water

Bay, which is also home to the Hong Kong University of Science and Technology.

Transport
The Eastern Harbor Tunnel puts Hong Kong Island's Sheung Wan–Causeway Bay corridor within comfortable commuting distance. The nearest MTR station is Hang Hau on the Tseung Kwan O Line. Taxis and minibuses can be scarce.

Advantages
Sai Kung and Clear Water Bay offer good value for money. The area's greenery, fresh air and low population density make it a pleasant place to live.

Drawbacks
Some villages are isolated and many residents need a car. There are a limited number of schools nearby. Village politics and ineffective law enforcement can be annoying.

Sha Tin

A large new town in the central section of the New Territories, Sha Tin is home to over 600,000 people.

Selection
Sha Tin includes medium- and high-rise apartment towers, detached and semidetached houses and public housing. Expect to pay $3.5 million for a 500-square-foot apartment. A 2,000-square-foot apartment costs $15 million, while villas and houses are $20 million–$30 million.

Amenities
Sha Tin has a good selection of shopping, restaurants and entertainment, including a concert hall and the Hong Kong Jockey Club's Sha Tin Racecourse. The area has numerous local schools, including the Chinese University of Hong Kong, and a public hospital.

Transport
Sha Tin is served by several stations on the MTR's East Rail Line, which runs between Shenzhen and Hung Hom. The Sha Tin to Central Link is now under construction and will ultimately connect Tai Wai

Station to Hung Hom and Admiralty. A well-developed highway network links Sha Tin to the rest of Hong Kong.

Advantages
Sha Tin is centrally located, has good access to China and Kowloon and offers good value for money.

Drawbacks
Until the Sha Tin to Central Link is operational, commuting to Tsim Sha Tsui or Hong Kong Island will be inconvenient. There are not many large, luxury homes in the area.

The south side

The south side comprises a range of neighborhoods and developments, including Chung Hom Kok, Deep Water Bay, Hong Kong Parkview, the Redhill Peninsula, Repulse Bay, Shek O, Shouson Hill, South Horizons, Stanley and Tai Tam. Some neighborhoods rival the Peak for exclusivity and many properties offer sea views.

The south side offers everything from individual houses to high-rise towers.

Selection
The south side includes luxurious high- and low-rise apartments, detached and semidetached houses, and large, self-contained residential complexes, such as Hong Kong Parkview. It also includes South Horizons, a mass-market development where four bedrooms are packed into a single 900-square-foot apartment. South side prices range from $4 million for a studio apartment to hundreds of millions of dollars for a detached house.

Amenities
Amenities vary with the neighborhood. Deep Water Bay and Shouson Hill are near the Hong Kong Country Club, the Hong Kong Golf Club and Ocean Park. Stanley is popular with tourists and offers shopping and waterfront dining. Hong Kong Parkview is an integrated complex with a well-stocked supermarket. Shek O has limited facilities but offers an attractive beach and a relaxed, village atmosphere. Many up-market developments have clubhouses and shuttle bus services.

Transport
The MTR does not serve the south side, although the South Island Line (East), which connects Admiralty to South Horizons with a stop at Ocean Park, is expected to open in 2016. The south side is well served by buses, minibuses and taxis.

Advantages
The south side offers an attractive combination of recreation, space, luxury, greenery and water views. From apartments to detached houses, there is something for everyone.

Drawbacks
The south side is linked to the rest of Hong Kong Island by narrow, twisting two-lane roads. A fallen tree, a landslide or a car accident can produce long traffic jams. In Stanley and other neighborhoods, tour buses are a nuisance. Shek O is far from major centers.

Taikoo Shing

Taikoo Shing is a collection of high-rise towers in Quarry Bay on the northeast side of Hong Kong Island. The site was formerly home to the Taikoo Dockyard.

Selection
This development comprises medium-sized apartments for Hong Kong's middle class. Expect to pay $10 million for a 600-square-foot apartment.

Amenities
Shopping, dining, schools and a public library are nearby. Some towers have swimming pools and other sports facilities.

Transport
There are two MTR stations in the area. Tai Koo is on the Island Line and Quarry Bay is an interchange between the Island Line and the Tseung Kwan O Line, which serves Sai Kung. Buses, minibuses and taxis are plentiful, and the Eastern Harbor Tunnel, which connects Hong Kong Island with Tsueng Kwan O, ends in Quarry Bay.

Advantages
Quarry Bay is emerging as a commercial hub as rents climb in Central and companies move their offices to the east side of Hong Kong Island. Apartments in Taikoo Shing are liquid, making them popular with investors. The area has excellent transportation links.

Drawbacks
This is a mass-market development and there are few large apartments. The development's design is functional rather than inspirational.

Union Square (West Kowloon)

Located on reclaimed land on the southwestern edge of the Kowloon Peninsula, Union Square incorporates the MTR's Kowloon Station, the Elements shopping mall and the International Commerce Center. Fifteen residential towers contain nearly 6,000 apartments, the oldest of which were built in 2000.

Selection
Residential towers in Union Square include The Arch, The Cullinan, The Harbourside, Sorrento and The Waterfront. Apartments range from about 400 to 1,500 square feet, with prices of $13 million–$75 million.

Amenities
Superb harbor views, balconies, clubhouses, gyms, swimming pools and function rooms are available in this development, which also includes the Ritz-Carlton and W hotels. Food and beverage outlets and shopping are available in the Elements mall. The West Kowloon Cultural District is being constructed nearby. Many multinational corporations have offices in the International Commerce Center.

Transport
Kowloon Station is underneath this development and is served by the MTR's Airport Express and Tung Chung lines. Austin Station on the MTR's West Rail Line is nearby, as is the West Kowloon Terminus for the express line to Shenzhen that is now under construction. The Western Harbor Tunnel, which connects Kowloon to Hong Kong Island, is adjacent to Union Square as are the West Kowloon Corridor and West Kowloon Highway.

Advantages
Apartments in Union Square are relatively new and well equipped. The location and transportation links make it convenient for people working at the airport or in Central. The new express rail link will soon provide convenient access to Shenzhen and Guangzhou.

Drawbacks
Apartments in Union Square are among the most expensive in Hong Kong. The Elements mall caters more to Mainland tourists than residents, making it easier to buy a designer handbag than a bag of carrots.

Western

Located on the northwest corner of Hong Kong Island, Western includes Sheung Wan, Sai Ying Pun, Shek Tong Tsui and Kennedy Town. This is an old district that is undergoing a renaissance.

Selection
Most of the homes in Western are new high-rise apartment towers, many of which offer harbor views, and older mid-rise blocks. A 200-square-foot studio apartment costs about $3 million, while a 1,300-square foot unit in a newer building costs $40 million.

Amenities
Western is being gentrified. Dried seafood shops in Sheung Wan are being replaced with art galleries, bistros and coffee shops. There is a new swimming pool in Kennedy Town and a pool and other athletic facilities at Sun Yat Sen Memorial Park in Sai Ying Pun.

Transport
New MTR stations opened at Hong Kong University, Sai Ying Pun and Kennedy Town in late 2014 and early 2015. Western is well served by buses and minibuses, including a rapid service to West Kowloon via the Western Harbor Tunnel. In 2013, a series of escalators on Center Street entered service, linking Bonham Road and the Sai Ying Pun Market.

Advantages
Western's main advantage is fast access to Central and other commercial districts. Western is less expensive than Mid-Levels, and there is a buzz that comes with an emerging neighborhood.

Drawbacks
The streets in Western are narrow, crowded and noisy. The area's metamorphosis is a work in progress and new luxury apartments like Harbor One are located next to old industrial buildings. There are very few large apartments.

SPECIAL CASES

OFF THE PLAN

In Hong Kong, buyers have a strong preference for new homes. In 2014, more than one-quarter of the homes that were sold were new. There are several reasons for this, including higher design and construction standards, better common facilities, such as swimming pools, and lower maintenance costs. It is also easier to obtain a mortgage loan for a new home.

Developers

Hong Kong has fewer than 30 large local companies that develop big residential projects (see the Developers section in the "Information Sources" chapter). In general, these companies are financially stable and don't leave projects half-finished or abscond with buyers' deposits. But large developers have failed. In 2003, two subsidiaries of a stock exchange–listed company that were building The Aegean and Villa Pinada in Tuen Mun entered receivership.[1]

Buyers are more likely to encounter smaller, less stable developers in the New Territories, where different rules apply. For example, designs for village houses do not need approval from the Buildings Department, and village houses can be erected without the services of an Authorized Person, such as an architect, surveyor or engineer. It is not unusual for indigenous villagers to illegally sell their building rights to a developer, who then sells the finished house to an outsider. These realities, coupled with the complexities of local politics, make due diligence essential for an off the plan purchase from a small developer in the New Territories.

In Hong Kong, property and related businesses have considerable political influence. The architecture, surveying and planning; engineering; finance; financial services; legal; and real estate and construction sectors each have a functional constituency seat in the Legislative Council. These seats ensure the industry's interests are represented, sometimes to the detriment of consumers.

Laws and misbehavior

Sales of new homes—including dwellings that are under construction and finished residences—are governed by the Residential Properties (First-hand Sales) Ordinance (Cap. 621), which took effect in April 2013. The ordinance was introduced to "promote the accuracy of market information and impose a discipline on the behavior of persons involved in selling" residential property. Anyone found guilty of violating the ordinance faces a fine of up to $5 million and a seven-year jail term. From April 2013 until June 30, 2015, however, no one has been prosecuted under the ordinance.[2]

The Sales of First-hand Residential Properties Authority (SRPA), which is the government body that was established to implement the ordinance, issues guidelines and practice notes. The authority's guidelines have legal effect and are admissible as evidence in court. However, there is no criminal or civil liability for not observing the guidelines, which cover operational issues, such as how and when vendors submit sales brochures and price lists to the SRPA. Practice notes are recommendations that have no legal effect. Failing to observe a practice note is not an offense under the ordinance. A typical practice note suggests that vendors ensure sales information is up to date and accurate.[3]

In November 2014, the Consumer Council issued a report on the ordinance's effect on sales practices. Entitled "Study on the Sales of First-Hand Residential Properties," the report observed that many questionable activities continued. For instance, one development's sales brochure comprised 594 pages, one-third of which were amendments, but the brochure failed to specify the amount of the monthly management fee. Salespeople offered buyers unofficial price lists they claimed had replaced the official versions and, to pressure people into buying, agents misrepresented the number of prospects who had registered their intent to purchase a home by up to 20 times. In one case, people who had won a lottery for the right to buy a home were given just three minutes to decide whether or not to make the purchase.

Sales materials

The ordinance lists the terms that must appear in the sale and purchase (S&P) agreement for a new home, the details to be included in the sales brochure and the timetable for making sales information public. A development's sales brochure should be available to the public at least seven days before sales begin, while the price list and sales arrangements should be available at least three days before the sale. The sales brochure should be no more than three months old.[4]

Descriptions of interior and exterior finishes, fittings and appliances are included in the sales brochure, as is information about how management fees are calculated. The brochure lists the public spaces and facilities in the development and explains the owners' responsibility for their management and upkeep as well as any obligation to maintain nearby slopes. It also includes a site plan, summaries of the preliminary S&P agreement and the deed of mutual covenant, the expected date that construction will be finished and the warranty, which is called the defect liability period.

In the sales brochure, the vendor is required to list any "relevant information." This is information that the developer has that is not known to the general public but that is likely to materially affect a buyer's ability to enjoy the property. Data in the Land Registry is considered to be public knowledge and does not have to be included in the "relevant information." Outline zoning plans, which are available from the Town Planning Board, provide useful information about the kinds of structures that can be erected near the development.

The sales brochure includes a cross-section plan that shows the elevation of units in the building in relation to nearby streets. This is important because developers have used creative floor numbering schemes to obscure a unit's actual elevation.

Only salable area can used to describe the size of a property in brochures, price lists and ads. Salable area is limited to the floor space inside a dwelling, plus the floor area of a balcony, a utility platform and a verandah, if these form part of the sale. Rooftops, parking spaces and gardens may not be included.[5]

You can obtain the salable area, age and permitted occupation purposes for domestic properties (other than New Territories village houses) from the Rating and Valuation Department's Property Information Online service, which also lists the ratable value of properties. In addition, the SRPA operates the Sales of First-hand Residential Properties Electronic Platform, an online database of sales brochures, price lists and transactions of first-hand residential developments.

The buying process

Buying off the plan is similar to buying an existing property—you sign a provisional S&P agreement, a formal S&P agreement and an assignment—but with several important differences.

After signing a provisional S&P agreement, you pay a preliminary deposit of 5% of the purchase price to the vendor. You then have five working days to execute a formal S&P agreement. Working days are days other than Saturdays, general holidays, or days on which the Signal 8 typhoon or black rainstorm warnings are in effect. If you do not execute the formal S&P agreement within five days, the provisional S&P agreement is terminated, you forfeit your 5% deposit and the vendor has no further claim against you.

If you execute the formal S&P agreement within five days, the vendor must execute the formal S&P agreement within eight working days of signing the provisional S&P agreement.

To protect your investment, the deposit check and subsequent payments are made to the solicitors' firm responsible for the project. The provisional and formal S&P agreements should include details about the fittings, finishes and appliances that are included in the sale.

You can appoint a solicitor and a real estate agent to represent your interests. You can also use the vendor's solicitor and agent, but this raises the possibility of a conflict of interest.

Vendors and their representatives are not allowed to accept expressions of interest before the price list is issued or before the sale of the properties begins.[6]

Construction delays

Delayed delivery is one of the most common problems with an off the plan purchase. The following information is from Schedule 5 of the Residential Properties (First-hand Sales) Ordinance and applies to unfinished buildings. Similar regulations govern developments that are complete but awaiting a certificate of compliance, which confirms that all positive obligations in the land lease, including the building covenant, have been fulfilled and an occupation permit has been issued. Developers cannot complete the sale of a new home until a certificate of compliance has been issued.[7]

The formal S&P agreement for a new home must include an estimated material date, which is the date that construction of the building is completed in all respects according to the building plans and complies with the development terms of the land grant.[8] The material date is also the day on which you complete the purchase of your new home.

The Authorized Person responsible for the project can extend the material date in the event of war, riot, strike or lock-out of workers, force majeure or act of God, fire or accident, or severe weather. If the Authorized Person extends the material date, the vendor has 14 days from the date that the extension is granted to give you a copy of the extension certificate.

If the vendor does not complete the building by the material date (or the extended material date, if an extension has been granted), you can cancel the contract. The cancellation must be in writing and the vendor has seven days to refund your deposit, plus interest. Interest is calculated at HSBC's prime rate plus 2% per annum. Repayment of your deposit plus interest represents "full and final settlement of all claims" against the vendor.

If the material date (or extended material date) passes and you do not cancel the purchase within 28 days, you are deemed to have agreed to wait for construction to be completed. You will be paid or receive credit for the interest on your deposit from the material date or extension date to the date when the project is finished.

If the development is not completed within six months of the material date (or extended material date), you can cancel the agreement and obtain a refund of your deposit with interest or wait for completion while interest continues to accrue.

Consent Scheme and Non-Consent Scheme sales

To protect buyers from developers going bankrupt before they have finished building a property, developers are prohibited from selling commercial, residential and industrial units before they are finished. There are two methods for overcoming this restriction: Consent Scheme and Non-Consent Scheme sales.

Vendors apply to the Director of Lands for permission to sell unfinished units under a Consent Scheme sale. With the director's approval, units can be sold subject to restrictions on the vendor's financing arrangements, the terms of the deed of mutual covenant, the timing and method of the sale, the contract format and the size of the buyer's deposit. In a Consent Scheme sale, the vendor's solicitor receives money from the purchaser and releases it to the vendor according to the terms of the scheme. Under the Consent Scheme, the vendor's solicitor may simultaneously represent the buyer, leading to a potential conflict of interest.

Non-Consent Scheme sales are regulated by the Law Society of Hong Kong. Under this arrangement, buyers pay the vendor's solicitor, who releases funds to the vendor according to the terms of the scheme. Failure to comply with the scheme constitutes a serious professional breach on the part of the solicitor. Non-Consent Scheme sales are commonly used when a developer demolishes and redevelops an existing building.

Completing the S&P agreement

Developers must apply for an occupation permit, a certificate of compliance or consent to assign from the Director of Lands within 14 days of construction being finished. When the occupation permit, certificate of compliance or consent to assign has been issued, the building is considered to be complete.

If a development is sold under the Consent Scheme, the vendor is required to notify you in writing that it can assign the property within one month of the issue of the certificate of compliance or the consent to assign, whichever happens first.

If a development is not subject to the Consent Scheme, the vendor is required to notify you in writing that it can assign the property within six months of the issue of the occupation permit.

Within 14 days of the vendor notifying you that they have received the occupation permit, certificate of compliance or consent to assign, you complete the S&P agreement. Usually, this happens at the office of the vendor's solicitor.

The Lands Department's Website lists developments that have been sold under the Consent Scheme as well as developments for which consent to sell and consent to assign have been issued.

Changes and defects

At completion, the vendor is responsible for ensuring that the home is as it was specified in the provisional and formal S&P agreements. That includes the fittings, finishes and appliances inside the home; the home's dimensions and location; and the communal and recreational facilities, such as swimming pools.

The vendor may amend the building plans, but must notify you within 14 days of receiving approval from the government. If the property's size changes, the price will be adjusted in proportion to the changes. But if the property's size increases or decreases by 5% or more, you can rescind the contract. After receiving notification of the change, you have 30 days to cancel the contract, at which point you receive all of your money back with interest, calculated using the formula outlined above. If you do not rescind the contract within 30 days, you are deemed to have accepted the changes.

If, due to factors beyond its control, the vendor is unable to deliver the fixtures, finishes or appliances specified in the S&P agreement, the vendor may substitute items of comparable quality.

Developers typically offer a six-month defect liability period on the components, fittings, finishes and equipment in a new home. However, some firms offer extended coverage. For example, in 2013, Sun Hung Kai Properties announced that it was introducing three-year warranties.[9]

Any defects in your new home should be reported to the vendor in writing. Repairs are generally made within two to four weeks, and defective items are only replaced as a last resort.[10]

Completed new homes

If you are buying a new dwelling that is completed (i.e., not under construction), the vendor should let you see the actual unit that you are buying or comparable home in the building. At the vendor's request, you can waive your right to view the residence. You are allowed to measure the home and shoot photos and video.

THE NEW TERRITORIES

The New Territories (NT) differs in many important ways from other parts of Hong Kong. This chapter explores the historical, political and legal realities that shape life and home ownership in the NT.

Britain leases the NT

Present day Hong Kong began in 1842 when China's Qing Dynasty ceded Hong Kong Island to Great Britain under the Treaty of Nanking. The Kowloon Peninsula was ceded to Britain in 1860 under the Convention of Peking. In 1898, Britain leased the New Territories for 99 years through the Convention for the Extension of Hong Kong Territory.

The NT comprises the land between Boundary Street in Kowloon and what is now known as the Shenzhen River and 235 outlying islands, including Lamma and Lantau.[1] When the lease was signed, the NT had 100,000 people and 800 villages. By 2014, the population had grown to 3.8 million and there were 709 officially recognized villages.

At 975 square kilometers, the NT dwarfs Hong Kong Island and Kowloon. The expiry of Britain's lease and the realization that Hong Kong would not be viable without the New Territories set the stage for Hong Kong's return to China in 1997.

When British administrators began exploring the New Territories in 1898, they received a hostile reception. Believing the colonizers would take their land and disrupt their way of life, villagers in Kam Tin pelted British administrators with eggs and didn't stop until 75 marines and two Maxim guns appeared. In 1899, a second uprising in Tai Po was crushed with cannon fire from British gunboats.[2]

In response to this hostility, the British adopted a policy of indirect rule. Sir Henry Blake—who had been the governor of Newfoundland, the Bahamas and Jamaica before arriving in Hong Kong in 1898—thought that the NT could not be managed in the same way as Hong Kong Island and Kowloon. Instead, he focused on collecting taxes and reassured residents that their "usages and good customs will not in any way be interfered with." As governor, Blake divided the New Territories into districts and sub-districts, which were managed by committees of village elders and overseen by a British district officer, who combined the roles of administrator, magistrate and chief of police.[3]

In 1905, the government passed the New Territories Land Ordinance (Cap. 97), which stated, "In any proceeding in Supreme Court in relation to land in the New Territories, the Court shall have power to recognize and enforce any Chinese custom or customary right affecting such land." This was in contrast to Hong Kong Island and the Kowloon Peninsula, where British property law was used and there was no recognition of traditional Chinese customs or rights.[4]

The Heung Yee Kuk

In 1924, a group of rural elites and clan leaders established the "New Territories Agriculture, Industry and Commerce Research Association." The group was recognized by the colonial government in 1959 with the passage of the Heung Yee Kuk Ordinance (Cap. 1097), as the highest statutory advisory body in the New Territories.[5] The official role of the Heung Yee Kuk (HYK) is to be "representative of informed and responsible opinion in the New Territories."

The HYK has 27 rural committees composed of village representatives who are elected by residents of indigenous villages. Previously, only indigenous villagers—the male descendants of men who lived in the village when the New Territories lease was signed in 1898—could vote. The franchise was later extended to women and to permanent residents of Hong Kong who have lived in a village for at least four years.[6] The HYK also has a functional constituency seat in Hong Kong's Legislative Council.

During the 1967 riots, the HYK played a key role in maintaining order in the New Territories, which was the scene of numerous clashes. In July 1967, for example, five Hong Kong police officers were killed when Chinese residents of Shau Tau Kok—a village that spanned the border with China—attacked a police post with bombs and automatic weapons.[7] To this day, the HYK's loyalty to the government and ability to mobilize rural communities give it enormous political clout.

The Heung Yee Kuk's influence grew under the leadership of Lau Wong-fat, the body's chairman from 1980 until 2015. As a member of the Basic Law Drafting Committee, Lau effectively guaranteed indigenous villagers' special status and the continuation of the Small House Policy. Article 40 of the Basic Law, which is Hong Kong's mini-constitution, states, "The lawful traditional rights and interests of the indigenous inhabitants of the New Territories shall be protected by the Hong Kong Special Administrative Region."[8]

In addition to being a powerful and skilled politician, Lau is wealthy. In 2010, as a member of Hong Kong's Executive Council, he confirmed that he owned 724 pieces of real estate. In June 2015, Lau Wong-fat's son, Kenneth Lau Ip-keung, was elected chairman of the HYK. He ran unopposed in the election.[9]

Urban planning in the New Territories is often chaotic.

Today, very little happens in the New Territories without the approval of the Heung Yee Kuk. The HYK has benefited indigenous villagers (and, ironically, helped them maintain a lifestyle that has vanished on the Mainland), but it has hampered efforts to make badly needed improvements to the NT's environment and urban planning. As the NT's non-indigenous population has increased, so have calls for an overhaul of the Small House Policy. A 2015 survey by Civic Exchange showed that nearly two-thirds of the public support or strongly support changing the policy.[10]

The Small House Policy

Until World War II, sons could build houses on land in NT villages. Government permission was required to build on agricultural parcels, and landless villagers could buy plots from the government. Over time, rising land prices made it increasingly difficult for villagers to build homes. Crown land was not granted to needy villagers. Instead, land was sold at public auction, where—in theory—anyone could buy it. Auctions at dawn and similar schemes prevented outsiders from buying village land.

In the late 1960s, village life was being disrupted by the industrialization and development of the New Territories. In 1971, at the request of the HYK, the government reviewed the village house policy. The following year, the Small House Policy (SHP) was introduced. Originally intended as a temporary measure, the SHP had three main ideas.

- ▲ It let a male indigenous villager over the age of 18 apply for permission to erect a small house for his own use on a suitable site within his village.[11]

- ▲ Land auctions would not be required, but for a small fee, land could be granted to indigenous villagers under private treaty grants.

- ▲ Village houses would be exempt from the Buildings Ordinance if they had a maximum covered area of 700 square feet (65 square meters), were less than 25 feet (8 meters) tall and had a maximum of two stories and a cockloft (a small garret). Houses could be built anywhere in the village, and professional oversight was not required.

The SHP has been amended several times since 1972. The maximum height was increased to two-and-a-half stories in 1974 and to three stories a year later. In 1976, villagers were prohibited from selling their houses to outsiders within five years of obtaining a certificate of compliance. (The certificate of compliance confirms that all positive obligations in the lease, including the building covenant, have been fulfilled and an occupation permit has been issued.[12]) In 1979, the non-assignment rule was modified to permit the sale of a house if the owner paid the full market premium to the government. In the 1980s, the 25-foot height restriction was increased to 27 feet.[13] In the 1990s, grant applicants were required to make a declaration to the District Lands Office that they intended to live in the house.[14] In 2006, the requirements for emergency vehicle access were relaxed. The next year, the Housing, Planning and Lands Bureau reaffirmed that villagers should not have a prior arrangement to transfer or dispose of their interest in land that they apply for under the SHP.[15]

Licenses, land grants and resales
There are three ways that an indigenous villager can build a village house:

▲ He can be granted a piece of land within his village or its environs under a private treaty grant.

▲ If he owns a suitable plot, he can be given a free building license to erect a village house. As its name suggests, no premium is payable under this method.

▲ If he owns unsuitable land, he can exchange it with the government for suitable land at a discounted price.

Each of these methods includes restrictions on reselling the home, which is also called alienation or assignment.

For example, private treaty grants have a perpetual restriction on alienation. If the home is inside a village expansion area, it cannot be resold during the first three years. From year four onward, it can be resold on payment of the full market premium. If the home is not in a village expansion area, it can be resold at any time on payment of the full market premium.

Under a free building license or land exchange, the house can be resold during the first five years on payment of the full market premium. After year five, no restrictions apply.

Small house problems

There are many issues surrounding small houses in the New Territories. For example, older homes built under the SHP frequently have leaking roofs and walls. Homes often lack insulation, and design challenges such as low ceilings, oddly positioned stairs and column-and-beam construction are common. In many older houses, the wiring, plumbing and drains need to be replaced. A wholesale renovation can easily cost $3 million.

The Small House Policy has been extensively criticized by the media, politicians and urban planners. The government announced that it would review the SHP in 2002, but little progress has been made.

Because it applies only to the male descendants of men living in NT villages in 1898, the SHP discriminates against non-indigenous villagers and women. The SHP is covered by an exemption in the Sex Discrimination Ordinance (Cap. 480). Outside the SHP, indigenous villagers are compensated more generously than their non-indigenous neighbors when the government expropriates land.[16]

Due to the open-ended nature of the SHP, there is no limit to the number of village houses that can be built. The amount of land in the New Territories, however, is finite. Furthermore, if the SHP was extended to female descendants of the original villagers, the problem would be even worse.

The government does not keep a list of indigenous villagers who are entitled to a small house grant, and only village heads can verify the eligibility of applicants. This creates opportunities for corruption. In January 2015, for instance, a developer and 11 indigenous villagers were charged with defrauding the Lands Department after they tried to bribe the head of a rural committee in Sha Tin in exchange for his help in obtaining 22 building licenses.[17]

Many villagers engage in speculation. Civic Exchange notes that the illegal sale of "ding" rights (indigenous villagers' right to build a home) is an open secret among government and interested parties. Depending on the village, the price of these rights ranges from $300,000 to $1 million.[18] The Audit Commission reported that between 1997 and 2002, 43% of the new homes built under the SHP had been resold.[19]

There are also questions about whether Article 40 of the Basic Law gives indigenous villagers a statutory right to a village house, as the HYK claims, or if the SHP is an administrative measure. In 2012, an indigenous villager living in Australia challenged the requirement that he live in a house obtained through the SHP. The judge ruled that the residency requirement was not unconstitutional.[20]

Special exemptions

Property in the NT is subject to several exemptions, some of which apply to all owners.

Village houses are exempt from rates, as long as the house is in an approved zone, called a designated village area, and meets the government's size and height restrictions. The exemption applies regardless of whether the home is occupied by an indigenous villager. Agricultural land is also exempt from rates.

Under Article 122 of the Basic Law, old schedule lots, small houses and similar rural holdings are exempt from increases in government rent as long as they are held by an indigenous villager.[21] Indigenous villagers also benefited from the New Territories Lease (Extension) Ordinance (Cap. 150), which extended leases expiring on June 30, 1997, until June 30, 2047. Under the ordinance, lessees did not have to pay a premium to extend their leases, but they did have to pay a new annual rent. Indigenous villagers are exempt from paying this rent.[22]

When the Small House Policy was introduced in 1972, there was a shortage of architects and contractors in the New Territories. To alleviate this problem, the government allowed houses to be built without the supervision of an Authorized Person or having the plans being approved by the Buildings Department.[23] These exemptions apply to all small houses in the NT—which are known as New Territories Exempt Houses—not just those owned by indigenous villagers. In some instances, such as homes built on sloping ground or multi-building developments, site formation and drainage plans may need to be approved before a house can be erected.

Unauthorized building works—including illegal additions and extra stories—are more likely to be tolerated in the NT than elsewhere in Hong Kong. The government has not conducted an official survey of the illegal structures in the NT, but estimates put the number at 35,000–200,000, with the situation in Yuen Long being particularly serious.[24] The Ombudsman investigated unauthorized building works in the NT in 1996, 2004 and 2011 and criticized the Lands Department and the Buildings Department for ineffective and inefficient enforcement of the regulations. Despite a high-profile crackdown that was announced in 2012, little progress has been made on this problem.

Local considerations

If you are thinking of living in the New Territories, check to see if your new home, neighborhood or village is affected by these issues.

Construction projects

The New Territories is a focal point for the government's housing and infrastructure development plans. Projects in Kwu Tung North, Fanling North, Ping Che/Ta Kwu Ling and Hung Shui Kiu are scheduled to start in 2018. Feasibility studies for converting industrial sites in North District, Yuen Long and Tuen Mun are now underway. The Lok Ma Chau Loop, near Shenzhen, has been identified as a potential development site, and work on the Liantang/Heung Yuen Wai Boundary Control Point should be finished in 2018. Construction of a columbarium, crematorium and related facilities at Sandy Ridge Cemetery is scheduled to start in 2016.[25]

The Mass Transit Railway's express rail link from West Kowloon to Shenzhen will operate in tunnels under Kam Shan, Tai Mo Shan, Kai Kung Leng and Mai Po. This project, which includes sidings in Shek Kong, is scheduled to be completed in 2018.[26]

Converted farmland

The 1905 Block Crown Leases contained a covenant specifying that agricultural land could not be used for other purposes without government approval.[27] This covenant was successfully challenged in a 1983 lawsuit in which the court held that landowners could use farmland for nonagricultural purposes that did not involve building. The ruling resulted in farmland being converted to storage yards for shipping containers, recycling facilities and automotive scrapyards. The government did not close this loophole until 1991, and anyone who had used their land for these purposes before 1991 was allowed to continue. While the storage, scrap and recycling facilities have been an economic boon for villagers, they have also created problems with traffic, noise and soil pollution. See the soil pollution section in the "Risks factors" chapter for details.

Environmental conflicts

Disagreements between conservationists and villagers are common. For instance, in 2014, villagers in Tai Ho on Lantau removed mangrove trees on private land that was zoned as a site of scientific interest and blocked an access path.[28] The same year, 200 villagers staged a protest against unfair land policies by clearing vegetation from a proposed conservation zone in a country park near Plover Cove.[29] In 2015, more than 27,000 objections were lodged with the Town Planning Board to stop indigenous villagers from building 26 homes in a country park near Uk Tau in Sai Kung.[30]

Feng shui

Feng shui (Chinese geomancy) addresses the harmonious arrangement of people, buildings and nature and is an important part of village life in the NT. *Feng shui* is subject to interpretation, and it can have a large impact on the price of a home or a parcel of land. Activities that disturb the local *feng shui* can also lead to substantial claims for damages. In 2010, the *South China Morning Post* reported that the Hong Kong government had paid $72 million in compensation to people whose *feng shui* had been upset by nearby construction projects.[31]

Graves

In urban parts of Hong Kong, people are encouraged to have their remains cremated. But in the NT, indigenous villagers have the right to a traditional burial. In 1983, the government introduced a policy allowing indigenous villagers to be buried on hillsides in what are known as permitted burial grounds. This policy has been widely abused, with unauthorized structures being erected, trees felled illegally and non-indigenous villagers interred in the permitted burial grounds. Environmental groups are concerned because many of the burial grounds are in or near country parks and conservation zones.[32]

This traditional New Territories grave is on Po Toi Island.

Roadblocks

As a result of poor urban planning, many access roads in the NT are built wholly or partially on private land. In 2015, residents of Siu Hang Hau in Clear Water Bay were told that they would have to pay a "maintenance fee" to use the only road to their homes.[33] A year earlier, the only road into Ho Chung New Village in Sai Kung was barricaded with concrete blocks and cement. It was the third such incident involving that road since 2009.[34]

Tsos and Tongs

The customary Chinese land rights recognized under the New Territories Land Ordinance include two traditional institutions, *Tsos* and *Tongs*, which are trusts based on ancestral ownership that hold a parcel or parcels of land for perpetuity. The manager of a *Tso* or *Tong* can sell its land, subject to the agreement of all the *Tso* or *Tong's* members and the approval of the Secretary for Home Affairs. In his book *Land Administration and Practice in Hong Kong*, Roger Nissim notes that the difficulty involved in obtaining unanimous approval makes the private purchase of *Tso* and *Tong* land "virtually impossible."

Vandalism and intimidation

Violence and threats are not uncommon in NT land disputes. In 2015, the head of a rural committee and a property agent were ordered to pay $1.4 million in compensation to an 85-year-old woman after they forced her off her farmland in Sheung Shui.[35] In 2014, protesters from the northeast New Territories scuffled with the police and broke windows in the Legislative Council building in response to the construction of two new towns that would displace the villagers from their homes.[36] Anyone interfering with village life, by opposing a land deal or the erection of a house, for example, is likely to find his car tires slashed.

Village life—A case study

In November 2014, I interviewed a couple who had purchased and renovated a village house in 2012. The interview went well and the following month I sent them a 1,000-word draft. As with case studies in previous books, I asked the couple to review the draft before it was published to ensure it was accurate and did not include any details that they would be uncomfortable making public.

I continued to work on other parts of the book while I waited for their comments. By early February, I hadn't heard anything, so I followed up. The couple then informed me that they did not want their case study to appear in the book.

In previous books, I have rewritten case studies to remove financial data and personal information. I've used pseudonyms and obscured the location of a property to protect the owner's privacy. When I offered to take these measures, the couple refused point-blank, fearing repercussions.

I was disappointed, but I respected their decision. That said, the couple experienced several problems that an outsider thinking of buying a village house should consider. For example:

▲ The couple were "asked" to pay the neighbors tens of thousands of dollars in compensation for the noise and inconvenience caused by their renovations. Work was halted for several weeks until the neighbors were paid.

▲ The neighbors have a flexible view of property boundaries. It is not unusual for the couple to come home and find the neighbors sitting on their patio.

▲ The couple pay a villager several hundred dollars each month to park their car on government-owned land. Car owners who refuse to pay have acid poured on their car.

▲ Like many village houses, the home included unauthorized building works that needed to be rectified.

These problems—and worse ones—are not unique to the couple's home. Before you buy a village house, learn about local issues and politics by doing an Internet search and talking to residents. And remember that the rules and their enforcement are different in rural parts of Hong Kong.

Mapping the New Territories

Shortly after the Convention for the Extension of Hong Kong Territory was signed in 1898, the area between Boundary Street and the Kowloon Hills became known as New Kowloon. This area was administered along with the urban parts of Hong Kong and enjoyed none of the special privileges of the NT.

One of the British government's first acts was to conduct a land survey so Crown rent—which is now called government rent—could be collected. Finished in 1904, the survey divided the NT into 477 demarcation districts, each of which was about 200 acres (81 hectares). A survey sheet was prepared for each district showing agricultural land, village houses and boundary features such as bunds, walls and fences. The Department of Land Surveying and Geo-Informatics at the Hong Kong Polytechnic University (HKPU) notes that the maps were less accurate in remote and built-up areas and that a "dimensional uncertainty of two to three meters would be expected." HKPU also observed large errors in some sheets. The orientation of some land parcels had shifted 90 degrees, and the position of others had moved more than 10 meters.[37]

While the survey was underway, the government began registering land claims. In 1900, land courts were established, where villagers could claim their property by producing proof of title, such as a deed of transaction. This was an imprecise process. Only some deeds were registered with the Chinese government, which did not maintain an index map of the registration records. Furthermore, to minimize their tax bill, landowners often understated the size of their holdings.

In 1905, the government issued a Block Crown Lease for each demarcation district. Attached to each lease was a survey sheet and a schedule listing the lot number, the name of the owner, the area and location of the lot, the class of the land and the Crown rent payable. The leases for these lots, which are now known as old schedule lots, had a duration of 75 years starting on July 1, 1898, with a right of renewal for an additional 24 years, less three days. In 1988, almost all of these leases were extended until June 30, 2047, through the New Territories Lease (Extension) Ordinance (Cap. 150).

Starting in 1906, building and agricultural lots were sold by auction. Known as new grant lots, these parcels were sold with a lease term of 75 years starting on July 1, 1898, with a right of renewal for an additional 24 years, less three days. These leases, which were also extended to 2047 under Cap. 150, included restrictions that were updated over the years in government gazette notices.

Schedules from the 1905 Block Crown Lease are still used to prove title for the sale of some village houses.[38] The survey sheets that accompany the schedules have been hand-traced and retraced over the years, introducing new errors. HKPU notes that the sheets "should not be taken as the sole reference" to define the boundaries of land parcels.

Inaccurate maps are just one potential problem with NT property records. For example, "missing lots" occur when the government cannot locate the boundaries of a lot that is properly registered in the block lease schedule. Some village houses were recorded collectively, not as individual house lots, in the 1905 survey sheets. Buildings frequently extend beyond a lot's boundaries, parcels have been extensively sub-divided and many lots overlap. Finally, records were destroyed during the Japanese occupation in World War II, making it impossible for the government to trace the original lease terms for some parcels. There are established procedures and legal precedents for addressing these issues, but this can consume large amounts of time, effort and money. An authorized surveyor, whose work is regulated by a code of conduct in the Land Survey Ordinance (Cap. 473), can help you spot and avoid problems.

NONRESIDENTIAL PROPERTY

Hong Kong offers a range of nonresidential investment opportunities, including industrial space, offices, parking spaces and retail space. These properties can be purchased for self-use, for income and for speculation.

Industrial space

At the end of 2014, Hong Kong had 17 million square meters of industrial space, which was evenly distributed between the urban areas and the New Territories. Much of the industrial space is left over from the days when Hong Kong was a light manufacturing center. Forty percent of the city's industrial space was completed before 1979 and more than 82% was built before 1989. Less than 6% was completed since 1994.[1]

Today, much of Hong Kong's factory space is used for warehousing, distribution and light industrial applications such as printing, commercial laundries, food factories and recycling. A substantial number of factories have been diverted to nonindustrial applications, such as furniture showrooms in Ap Lei Chau, private kitchens in Wong Chuk Hang, art galleries in Chai Wan and artists' studios in Tai Po. Many flatted factories have been turned into apartments. These nonindustrial uses are usually in violation of the outline zoning plan, occupation permit or government land lease, but they are widely tolerated.

Hong Kong's industrial spaces differ from lofts in cities such as New York and London, where architectural details like pressed-tin ceilings, hardwood floors, ornate ironwork and elaborate masonry are common. While some local factories offer large windows and high ceilings, most are concrete boxes that were erected as quickly and cheaply as possible.

Slumping property values after the Asian financial crisis in 1997 and the migration of Hong Kong's factories to southern China left many owners in negative equity and unwilling to spend money on anything except essential repairs. As a result, water leaks, uneven floors, antiquated elevators and spalling concrete are common.

Many industrial units are owned by investors who are waiting for the building or neighborhood to be redeveloped. Units are often left empty, because rents are low and it's easier to sell without a tenant. Even if the unit is tenanted, many owners refuse to spend money on repairs that have been approved by the owners' corporation. Lawsuits are frequently used to force owners to pay for essential repairs to electrical systems and leaking roofs.

Factory buildings can be noisy, especially if your neighbors are making things. There are also health and safety concerns, such as the lack of fire sprinklers in older buildings and the toxic chemicals that were—and continue to be—used in many buildings. Industrial units are sold on an "as-is" basis and there are no guarantees that chemicals that were used on the premises have been properly cleaned up.

Heating and air-conditioning is also a consideration. High ceilings and large, open spaces are expensive to heat and cool. You may want to budget for internal partitions.

Compared with apartments, non-Chinese owners are relatively rare in industrial buildings. Owners' corporation meetings are usually held in Cantonese, and if you are not bilingual, you'll need to send someone in your place or let the natural stinginess of your co-owners prevail.

Finally, some areas, such as Wong Chuk Hang, have seen prices spike as developers replace factories with hotels and office buildings. Despite these changes, banks tend to be conservative when valuing industrial properties for mortgages.

Offices

At the end of 2014, Hong Kong had more than 11 million square meters of office space. More than half of the space was in Sheung Wan, Central, Wanchai, Causeway Bay and Tsim Sha Tsui. As prices rise, however, office space is being built in noncore areas such as Kwun Tong and Wong Chuk Hang. Forty percent of Hong Kong's office space was built before 1990, 38% was erected in the 1990s and the remaining 22% was constructed since 2000.

Offices in older buildings generally sell for less than those in newer ones, which are more energy-efficient and require less maintenance. Other factors that affect prices include the proximity to Central—where Hong Kong's most expensive offices are located—and the Mass Transit Railway, the quality of the neighborhood and the presence of sea views.

Hong Kong offices are divided into three categories. Grade A buildings have central air-conditioning, large floor plates, parking, multiple elevators and attractive lobbies. Grade A buildings such as International Finance Center and Exchange Square comprised 64% of the total in 2014 and are usually well managed.

Grade B buildings, which made up 23% of the total in 2014, may have central air-conditioning and parking, and have a less glamorous lobby. Grade B offices can be attractive, but are not as large, luxurious or well equipped as Grade A.

Grade C buildings don't have parking or central air-conditioning, may only have one elevator and have a basic lobby. Grade C offices may have a floor plate of 500–600 square feet (46–56 square meters) and are popular with cost-conscious tenants.

The quality of property management in Grade B and C buildings, where most small businesses operate, is variable. In Grade C buildings, it is not unusual to find a security guard asleep on a cot in the hallway on weekends or for the building to be closed on Sundays. The building's location does not determine its grade: There are Grade A buildings, such as Nina Tower, in Tsuen Wan and Grade C buildings in the back streets of Central.

A large proportion of Hong Kong's Grade A buildings are owned by big landlords, such as Hongkong Land, and rented out. Most Grade A office transactions are en bloc (whole building) sales, but there are some buildings, such as Bank of America Tower in Central and Lippo Center in Admiralty, where it is possible to buy individual units at approximately $30,000 per square foot ($323,000 per square meter). The sale of floors and individual offices is far more common in Grade B and C buildings, where prices start at about $10,000 per square foot.

If you are buying an office for investment purposes or for your own use, keep the following points in mind.

▲ Carefully check the operation and cleanliness of common facilities, like fire exits and shared bathrooms. Some Grade B and C buildings do not provide toilet paper or hand towels.

▲ Pay attention to the quality of maintenance and upkeep in older buildings. Replacing elevators, air-conditioning systems and roofs can be very expensive.

▲ Check the lobby directory to see what kinds of businesses are in the building. Unlicensed private clubs, restaurants and even one-person brothels are not unusual in Grade B and C buildings.

▲ Some buildings only permit renovations by a single contractor who has been approved by the management committee. This arrangement can make renovations costly.

▲ Alterations to the fire sprinkler system can only be made by licensed contractors, who are also expensive.

▲ The central air-conditioning in older Grade A and B offices may struggle to cool the building during July and August, particularly if the owners have deferred repairs.

▲ Many buildings operate their central air-conditioning from 08:00 or 08:30 until 18:30 or 19:00 on weekdays and from 08:00 to 13:30 on Saturdays, and charge $300+ per hour (often with a two- or three-hour minimum charge) to turn the system on after hours. These buildings are often sealed, making it uncomfortable to work without the air-conditioning. The individual air-conditioning in a Grade C office can be very convenient if you work unusual hours.

Parking spaces

Car parking spaces are a relatively inexpensive, low-maintenance way to invest in Hong Kong real estate. Prices range from under $1 million to over $4 million per space and banks will provide mortgages. Prices are affected by the age and location of the building and by the supply of parking nearby. Owners of parking spaces are liable for rates and management fees and for special assessments if the building is being renovated. Most real estate agencies handle parking spaces. Information is also available from ParkingHK.com (www.parkinghk. com).

Retail space

At the end of 2014, Hong Kong had 11 million square meters of retail space, about 30% of which was on Hong Kong Island, 30% in Kowloon and 40% in the New Territories. Two-thirds of the city's retail space was built before 1990, 22% in the 1990s and the remaining 13% since 2000.

Hong Kong has a thriving market for retail space. Compared with North America, most units are relatively small, typically less than 2,500 square feet (232 square meters). Prices, however, can be very high, especially for street-level outlets in shopping areas like Causeway Bay.

RENOVATIONS

PLANNING AND STAFFING YOUR PROJECT

In Hong Kong, buying a property is often only the first step. You'll want to renovate it, too.

You will renovate for several reasons. One is that some of the more interesting properties are older and have had only minor improvements over the years. New wiring and plumbing are often essential. Combining smaller rooms and installing energy-efficient, double-glazed windows and split-type air conditioners can also make a big difference.

The high cost of property is another reason to renovate. If you spend millions of dollars on a property, you won't want to skimp on the personal touches that turn someone else's apartment into your home.

That said, you should carefully consider the costs in time, money and frustration before starting a major renovation project. You may conclude that buying a new home or one that has already been refurbished makes more sense than renovating an existing one.

Defining the project

Start by assembling a wish list of everything that you'd like in your new home. Think about the features and design elements you've admired in hotels, resorts, friends' homes and previous places where you have lived. If you've always wanted a Jacuzzi, a craft room or a home theater, then add them to your list. If you are concerned about personal security, consider adding alarm and surveillance systems.

This is a good time to consult interior design books and magazines, like *Architectural Digest* and *Better Homes and Gardens*. Sites like ArchDaily (www.archdaily.com) and Architizer (www.architizer.com) are also helpful. Local interior design magazines can be a source of inspiration, even if you can't read Chinese.

Design books, magazines and Websites are an inexpensive way to spur your imagination. They will also provide nonverbal ways of communicating your ideas to the designer or contractor. This can be useful if there is a gap between your Cantonese skills and the designer's English abilities. You can combine photos, magazine pages, paint chips and fabric swatches on a foam board to create palettes of colors, textures and styles.

The purpose of this process is to help you consider all of the possibilities. You may not act on them, but it is much easier and less expensive to make changes at this stage than when work is underway. You may also find that something that you've always dreamed of—a home spa, for example—is not that much more expensive than a conventional bathroom.

Designers vs. contractors

If you have the time and inclination to take a hands-on approach, you can hire a general contractor directly. This choice is cost-effective if you know what you want, the design requirements of your project are relatively limited and you don't need help with furniture and fabrics. Eliminating the designer can save 10% to 20% of the renovation cost, assuming everything goes according to plan.

Many contractors in Hong Kong speak English and use computer-aided design software that will help you visualize your finished project.

This approach, however, has drawbacks. For example, the contractor may not speak English fluently, which probably won't be an issue when you are discussing bricks, but could be when deciding on a shade of paint. Designers often give you more and varied options and they can have more adventuresome tastes.

You will pay the contractor a design and construction fee and a mark-up on the goods and services they provide for your project.

For most people, hiring a designer or architect is a better solution. The added cost is usually offset by the designer's technical knowledge, problem-solving and project management skills and relationships with contractors and suppliers. It is much easier to hire a designer at the beginning of a project than to find someone to rescue a job that has encountered problems.

The designer typically offers a turnkey package that includes overall project management, obtaining permits and approvals, specifying and sourcing construction materials and overseeing the construction team. The designer hires a contractor, who provides the tradespeople, like electricians, painters and masons, necessary to complete the job. The designer can also recommend or specify appliances as well as the furniture, drapery and accessories needed to give your home a completed look.

A talented designer can anticipate and avoid problems. She will interpret and refine your ideas, make time- and money-saving suggestions and help you overcome any limitations that your property has, like low ceilings or unusual room layouts. She can also save you time by bringing material samples to your home or office.

The cost of a renovation will be determined by several factors, including the condition of the home; the quality of the materials; whether the project involves extensive demolition and structural changes; whether furniture and appliances are included; and the popularity of the designer.

Given the number of variables involved, budgets vary widely. The designer will typically charge you a price per square meter, with an hourly charge for time spent on site. Some designers will quote on a lump-sum basis.

Evaluating designers

When you have a clear idea of your needs, it's time to start shopping for a designer. Friends, coworkers and neighbors are excellent sources of information and referrals. Lifestyle magazines often feature designers' projects, as does the Sunday magazine in the *South China Morning Post*. Trade groups for architects and designers are listed in the "Information sources" chapter.

Once you've located some candidates, you'll want to evaluate their suitability for your project. This is a three-part process based on chemistry, workmanship and money.

Chemistry
Your relationship with the designer will contribute to the project's overall success. Find someone with whom you can communicate and who understands your tastes and sensibilities. Trust and respect will help you overcome the challenges and setbacks that inevitably occur.

The designer should be comfortable with your level of involvement in the project. Some clients are hands-on and want to make site visits and shop for bathtubs, hardware and furnishings. Other customers prefer to leave everything up to the designer.

The designer must be reliable about keeping appointments and other commitments. Initial difficulties here can foreshadow bigger problems later on.

There's no substitute for spending time with the designer to get a sense of her personality. Interviewing her clients, seeing her work and asking the questions outlined below will provide insights into the designer's strengths and weaknesses.

While you're asking the following questions, consider the client's personality. Is he easygoing or a perfectionist? Did he change his mind several times during the course of the project or pick one design and complete it? An overly demanding or unreasonable client can undermine the work of even the most professional designer.

▲ What was the designer like to work with?

▲ Was she open to your ideas and suggestions?

▲ Did she complete the project on schedule and on budget? If not, why?

▲ What did you like most (and least) about working with the designer?

▲ Were you happy with the quality of the materials and workmanship? If not, why?

▲ If you had the renovation to do over again, what would you do differently?

▲ How much did you spend?

Workmanship

You're going to spend a substantial amount of money on your renovation, so it's important that you're happy with the finished product. The easiest way to do this is to inspect an example of the designer's work. For maximum candor, this should be done while the designer is not present.

If possible, inspect a project that is several years old, so that you can see how the materials and workmanship have aged. Pay close attention to cabinetry, floors and custom woodwork. Check that the doors and shelves are hung straight and that floors and countertops are level. Look for water leaks and inspect the quality of the finishes. Ask plenty of questions, take notes, and if the owner doesn't mind, bring along a digital camera. You may see something interesting that you'll want to incorporate into your own design.

Money

Quality costs money, and good designers and contractors are usually in demand and able to charge premium prices. That said, companies price projects differently for a variety of reasons, including their current workload, the market outlook, how interesting the project is, the project's potential to generate referrals or media coverage and whether they are working on a job nearby.

Get several quotes, and pick the company that has the optimum combination of chemistry, workmanship and price. If you like the people and the workmanship, but the price seems high, ask why. The designer or contractor may be basing her price on an incorrect assumption, or there may be something that you can do to bring the price into your budget.

Naturally, you will want to get the lowest possible price. But allow the designer some profit, particularly if you have high expectations or the project is complex. Otherwise, the designer may cut corners to ensure that the job is profitable, or be slow to fix problems later on.

Hiring a designer

▲ Create a shortlist of designers who meet your criteria.

▲ Brief them on the project and ask for a preliminary quote.

▲ Get at least three quotes to ensure that the prices are competitive. Ensure that the quotes include comparable materials and services.

▲ Evaluate the quotes and pick a designer.

▲ The designer will prepare a contract with completion dates, project scope and a payment schedule. The contract should also specify how and where disputes will be settled and the liquidated damages that will be paid if either party fails to fulfill the contract. Have a lawyer review the contract before you sign it, especially if it is a large project.

▲ When you've settled on one company and are confident you can work with them, advise the others that their bids were unsuccessful.

▲ After you have signed the contract, you will pay a deposit. You will also make payments as the project progresses.

▲ There will be a final payment to the contractor, typically 5% of the total, that is held back for up to a year after the project is completed. This payment protects you in case there are defects in the materials or workmanship and covers the cost of fixing common, minor problems like cracks that appear in plaster as it dries.

Making the project a success

There are several things that you can do to increase the chances that your project will be a success.

⏶ Conduct due diligence. Ensure the designer takes pride in her work, doesn't cut corners on materials and workmanship and has the skills and resources to complete the project. In addition to talking to previous clients, you can hire a lawyer or an investigator to do a background check. This may seem like a lot of work, but it's nothing compared to the time and trouble needed to extricate yourself from a project that has gone wrong.

⏶ Have a realistic budget and timetable. You won't be happy with the results if you insist on an impossibly tight schedule, have a tiny budget or use cheap materials. Don't forget to allow for contingencies and delays.

⏶ Treat the designer well. Pay your bills, recognize that there will be unforeseen problems and make decisions in a timely fashion.

⏶ Older Hong Kong buildings are notorious for design and construction quirks. Often, floors aren't level, walls aren't true and corners aren't square. While some of these issues can be overcome, others cannot and some problems will not be apparent until work starts. Usually the cost and difficulty involved mean that compromises will need to be made.

⏶ Have reasonable expectations and communicate them clearly. Your expectations may be unrealistic—or impossible—for your budget, building or schedule. Or they could be delivered with a few adjustments. But if the designer doesn't know what you want, it isn't going to happen.

⏶ Remember that designers and contractors depend on a network of people and businesses. Good contractors and designers work with reliable suppliers because their livelihoods depend on it. But problems can occur when workers don't show up, materials aren't delivered on time, etc. There are times when you will have no choice but to simply roll with the punches.

⏶ Get covered. Make sure the project is covered by your homeowners' insurance, a separate rider or the designer or contractor's policy. Ensure that all tradespeople are covered by workers' compensation insurance.

▲ Stay organized. Use a filing system for the signed contract, drawings, permits, insurance policies, receipts, notes, photos, instruction manuals, model and serial numbers and warranty information for appliances, and catalog numbers for paints and floor coverings. Scan and keep backup copies in the cloud, using a service like Dropbox. Having this information organized will make life much easier if there is a dispute or if you need to arrange repairs or renovations at a later date.

▲ Move out. Living in a home that is being renovated can expose you and your family to unhealthy levels of dust, noise and stress, and delay the project's completion. It's often cheaper to put your possessions into storage and live in a serviced apartment, a sublet or an Airbnb rental.

APPROVALS AND PERMITS

Renovations in Hong Kong may require two sets of approvals.

Your owners' corporation

The first approval, which comes from the owners' corporation, is for alterations listed in your building's deed of mutual covenant. Typically, this involves changes to common areas, such as the lobby, and to the building's exterior. For instance, you may have to match the size and shape of new windows to those of your neighbors. You may also need approval for changes to non-load-bearing walls inside your apartment.

In addition, you will need to register your contractor with the building's management company and ensure that he abides by the house rules, which cover issues such as identity cards for tradespeople, permitted working hours, transporting building materials in passenger elevators, etc. You will also pay a deposit to the owners' corporation or the management company to cover any damage that the contractor causes to common areas. The deposit, which typically ranges from $3,000 to $20,000, is refunded two to six weeks after the project is completed, if there was no damage.

The Buildings Department

The second set of approvals is from the Buildings Department (BD). Large projects, for example work involving load-bearing structures, require the prior approval of the BD and the appointment of an Authorized Person (AP), such as an engineer, architect or surveyor, who is registered with the government. Depending on the project, you may also need to appoint a registered structural engineer or a geotechnical engineer. The AP designs and supervises the work, which is carried out by a registered contractor. The BD's Website includes lists of registered APs, inspectors, structural engineers, geotechnical engineers and contractors, including general building contractors, specialist contractors and minor works contractors.

The Minor Works Control System

On December 31, 2010, the government introduced the Minor Works Control System, which divides 126 smaller projects into three classes.[1] Class I covers complex projects, such as building or altering solid walls less than five meters tall and repairs to underground drains. Class II encompasses less complex work, like repairs to windows or walls containing windows. Class III includes minor projects, like erecting or removing a clothes drying rack.

For Class I projects, you must appoint an AP and a structural or geotechnical engineer, if necessary, as well as a registered contractor to carry out the work. For Class II projects, you can appoint a registered contractor, without an AP. At least seven days before Class I or II projects begin, a MW01 or MW03 form, along with project details and plans, must be filed with the BD. Within 14 days of completion, a MW02 or MW04 form must be filed with the BD.

For Class III works, you can hire a registered contractor. Within 14 days of the project's completion, a MW05 form must be filed with the BD. There is no need to appoint an AP or to notify the BD before work starts.

Registered minor works contractors are divided into seven types, depending on their specialization: Type A specializes in alterations and additions; B in repairs; C in signboards; D in drainage; E in structures for amenities; F in finishing; and G in demolition.

Certain activities, such as hanging wallpaper and interior plastering and painting, are exempt from the Minor Works Control System. However, some projects can occupy multiple categories. Depending on a canopy's height, size and material, it could be in Class I, II or III, or it could be exempt.

The person who arranges the work—whether they are a property owner, an occupant or an agent—is legally required to hire an AP or a registered contractor, as appropriate. Anyone who knowingly fails to hire an AP or a registered contractor can be fined up to $100,000. Contractors who certify work outside their area of expertise can be jailed for six months and fined $5,000 per day that the offense continues.[2]

Under the Minor Works Control System, clothes drying racks, air conditioner frames and small canopies that were installed without prior permission from the Building Department can be retained if a qualified inspector determines that they are safe. This program is known as the Household Minor Works Validation Scheme.

An illegal balcony

In early 2009, the Buildings Department (BD) hired a contractor to inspect the balconies in our building. On March 6, 2009, the BD issued a statutory order that named our balcony as one of 144 in the complex that were unauthorized building works. We were given until May 4 to fix the balcony. Following an application by our owners' corporation, the deadline was extended until September 30, 2009.

In May 2009, we learned that we had four options.

1. We could have the balcony inspected by an Authorized Person (AP). If the AP felt the balcony was structurally sound, we could apply to the BD for what amounted to a waiver.

2. If the balcony failed the inspection, the AP would recommend corrective action and we could apply to the BD for "acceptance" of those repairs. With options 1 and 2, the balcony would still be an unauthorized building work, but it would be tolerated by the BD and the statutory order would be lifted. If there was a change in the balcony's structural condition or in the BD's enforcement policy, however, the statutory order could be reinstated.

3. We could return the balcony to its original design or rebuild it to the BD's current standard. After the balcony was reinstated, we could leave it alone or apply for permission to rebuild the balcony using a new, BD-approved design.

4. We could apply to the BD for permission to demolish the balcony and rebuild it according to a new design that the BD had approved.

Options 3 and 4 would result in the statutory order being lifted and the balcony would no longer be an unauthorized building work.

We chose option 1. In September 2009, an AP inspected our balcony and found it unsatisfactory.

Before the repairs.

In December 2009, we joined a group of affected owners and hired a firm of consulting engineers to review the situation. In early January 2010, we received a notice from the BD that it intended to prosecute us. If convicted, we faced a fine of $200,000, one year in jail, and $20,000 for each day that we failed to comply with the statutory order. Two weeks later, we learned that, based on an application by the consulting engineers, the BD had given us another extension—until April 30, 2010—to make the necessary repairs.

Things were quiet until February 2013, when we discovered that a neighbor had received a summons for failing to fix his balcony, which was one of the 144 identified in 2009. His court date was set for the following month.

The floor, rails and glass panels are removed.

Halfway through the renovation. The glass panels will sit in the steel channels on the right.

At this point, we had not heard from the BD in more than three years. We assumed the consulting engineer was handling the situation and that, if we just waited for instructions, everything would be fine.

When we learned of our neighbor's summons, we contacted the consulting engineer and discovered that he had done nothing with our file. With help from our building's management office, we hired a registered general contractor and, in February 2013, paid a $48,000 deposit against a final cost of $119,000. The contractor appointed an AP and a structural engineer on our behalf and on March 6, 2013, the structural engineer submitted drawings for option 4. The BD approved the drawings on May 3 and suspended its case against us.

On June 3, 2013, scaffolding was erected. The balcony floor and glass panels were removed on June 6 and the project—which also included excavating and refilling a recessed planter, replacing two drain pipes and repairs to spalling on the balcony ceiling—was completed on August 7. The scaffolding stayed up for a further two weeks to accommodate any unexpected problems. The long construction period was the result of bad weather, family holidays and additional approvals from the BD.

On May 12, 2014, the BD inspected the balcony. On March 20, 2015, we received notification from the BD that the work had been completed satisfactorily. We paid the remaining $4,800 to the contractor, which had been held back pending the BD's final approval.

The finished balcony.

The new contractor was a major improvement over the consulting engineer, but there were two issues. First, the project required the replacement of most of the balcony floor, but a match for the existing floor tile could not be found. It never occurred to us that the contractor (or any apartment owner, for that matter) would accept unmatched tile. As a result, we paid an additional $7,800 for labor and materials to have the entire floor retiled. We also had to call the contractor back several times to remove stray grouting.

Throughout this process, our management committee was actively involved and supportive. They helped us find engineers and other professionals, met representatives from the BD to clarify its position and researched and shared solutions, so one owner would not have to repeat the work of his neighbor. The committee was not obliged to provide any of these services and could have left individual owners to their own devices.

LOCAL CONSIDERATIONS

Air conditioners

Hong Kong's hot, humid climate makes air-conditioning essential. Central air-conditioning systems are rare in residential buildings and many older apartments have window-type units, which are noisy and inefficient. Replacing window-mounted models with split-type air conditioners reduces the noise level inside the apartment and saves energy. Many manufacturers offer split-type models with built-in heaters, which are called reverse-cycle or inverter air conditioners. This feature is useful during Hong Kong's cool winter months. It also lets you dispense with the electric heaters that are underfoot for the rest of the year.

Under the Ozone Layer Protection Ordinance (Cap. 403), Hong Kong is ending the import of products containing hydrochlorofluorocarbons (HCFCs). Used as a refrigerant in air conditioners, HCFCs are being phased out on the following schedule:

- On July 1, 2012, all products containing chlorodifluoromethane (HCFC-22) were banned.

- On January 1, 2015, all products containing HCFCs, except dichlorotrifluoroethane (HCFC-123) were banned.

- On January 1, 2020, all products containing HCFCs will be banned.[1]

As a result of the legislation, you may have to replace an otherwise serviceable air conditioner because you cannot replace the refrigerant that has been lost due to leakage or repairs. You may also have to replace the pipe connecting the outdoor condenser with the indoor fan unit.

If you buy a split-type air conditioner directly from one of the major manufacturers, the company will provide technicians to install the equipment but they will not arrange the scaffolding needed to install the condenser unit. An air-conditioning contractor can supply labor, equipment and scaffolding. Ensure that you and the contractor have adequate public liability and workers' compensation insurance.

Bamboo scaffolds are often used when technicians install condensers for split-type air conditioners.

Your air conditioner's condenser must be fitted with a proper drain. Filters on the fan units should be cleaned regularly to ensure that the air conditioners work properly and don't waste electricity.

Consumables

Before buying appliances, check the price and availability of consumables, such as water filters. Consumables can be expensive and hard to find, particularly if they are imported and sold by one supplier.

Disputes

Disputes between contractors or designers and their clients are common in Hong Kong. Sometimes practitioners take on too much work, fail to adequately supervise workers, use poor quality materials and ignore deadlines. At other times, customers make endless changes, refuse to pay or otherwise antagonize the contractor and tradespeople.

These disputes can become unpleasant. Tempers fray, positions harden and a designer or contractor will abandon a job. Other companies are usually reluctant to step in, adding to the cost and time required to complete the project. This situation is stressful for the customer, who is left paying rent on one home, paying a mortgage on a second and dealing with rapidly escalating costs.

Disputes may be resolved in court, leading to a legal bill on top of the designer or contractor's invoice. More frequently, your solicitor and the practitioner's solicitor will exchange letters until an agreement is reached. Occasionally, a contractor will resort to vandalism or violence.

You can avoid many problems by picking good suppliers and maintaining a cordial relationship with them. Sometimes, the "least worst" option is to pay to make a problem go away, even if you are in the right. Ultimately, almost anything is preferable to an abandoned project or a lawsuit.

Electricity

If you buy an older apartment, you may need to upgrade the electrical system.

Many older homes have too few power outlets. The 2009 edition of the Code of Practice for the Electricity (Wiring) Regulations recommends at least one outlet per 1.2 square meters of floor space in the kitchen, one for every 2.5 square meters in the living room and dining room and one for every 3 square meters in the bedrooms. At a minimum, there should be three outlets in the kitchen, four in the living room and dining room and two in each bedroom.

Older apartments often have ungrounded, two-pin power outlets; large and small three-pin outlets (British BS 546 standard); and the three-blade outlets (BS 1363) that are now standard in Hong Kong.

The breaker panel may also need to be replaced with a new miniature circuit breaker, which protects against current overloads and short circuits. Miniature circuit breakers include residual current devices (RCDs) that immediately disconnect the power when electricity leaking to ground is detected. RCDs can prevent electrical fires and lethal shocks, particularly in places like kitchens and bathrooms, where water and electricity are in close proximity.

Hong Kong's electrical code also specifies that:

▲ Circuit breaker panels must be labeled to indicate the circuit controlled by each breaker.

▲ In a bathroom, switches and other electrical controls should be inaccessible to a person using a bath or shower. Electrical outlets installed in a bathroom must be at least 60 centimeters from a shower, sink or bathtub. Elsewhere, outlets should be installed as far away as practicable from water taps, gas taps or cooking ranges.

▲ Outdoor lights, power outlets and switches must be weatherproof.

When your renovation is complete, the contractor will issue a WR1 or WR1(A) form, indicating that the installation has been inspected, tested and certified by a registered electrical worker.

Energy conservation

CLP—the electrical utility that serves Kowloon, the New Territories and the outlying islands except Lamma—has started trials of smart electricity meters. If you are thinking of installing a smart meter, review the Electronic Frontier Foundation's reports about privacy concerns surrounding these devices.

Compact fluorescent lamps and light-emitting diode (LED) lamps are more energy-efficient than their halogen and incandescent counterparts. They also produce less heat, reducing demand on your air conditioner.

Smart controls, such as timers and automatic light sensors, can minimize wasted electricity. Home automation systems are more expensive but offer even greater control.

Most Hong Kong residents live in apartments, making green rooftops, photovoltaic cells and solar water heaters impractical, although these technologies can be deployed in some village houses.

Floors

Hong Kong's high humidity makes wall-to-wall carpeting impractical. Instead, most apartments have ceramic tiles in the kitchen and bathrooms and hardwood floors elsewhere. Marble is also used, although it can be slippery when wet.

In a renovation, the existing flooring can sometimes be retained after it has been sanded to remove dents and gouges and then stained and resealed. If you replace the wood floors, you have two choices: solid hardwood or manufactured flooring.

Hardwood flooring is sold in strips of varying widths and lengths and is usually milled using an interlocking, tongue-and-groove system. Many varieties are available, including traditional woods such as oak and teak, environmentally friendly hardwoods from sustainable forests and exotic woods from Africa and South America. Solid wood is durable and can be sanded and refinished several times before it must be replaced. Solid hardwood expands and contracts with varying humidity and can buckle and warp if the home is flooded. To minimize noise, a layer of cork can be installed between the wood and the concrete underneath.

Manufactured flooring has a wood veneer on top, a shock- and sound-absorbent layer in the middle and an underlay on the bottom. This flooring is manufactured to a high tolerance and is less likely to buckle and warp. However, the relatively thin wood veneer limits the number of times this material can be resurfaced.

Regardless of whether you use hardwood or manufactured flooring, select a mainstream product from an established manufacturer. That will make it easier to match your existing flooring in case of repairs. If you want perfectly flat, gap-free floors, explain this to your contractor or designer before work starts.

Gas

Gas is a popular fuel for cooking and water heaters. Throughout Hong Kong, gas is supplied by the Hong Kong and China Gas Co., also known as Towngas.

If you are renovating, Towngas or one of its contractors will install new gas pipes as well as gas-powered appliances, such as ovens, clothes dryers and water heaters. Towngas also sells appliances and kitchen systems.

Heritage properties

Hong Kong has very few heritage properties, so preservation orders are unlikely to be an issue for most homeowners.

Holidays

Many contractors work from Monday to Saturday. However, renovations stop over the Lunar New Year holidays, when many people return to their ancestral villages on the Mainland. This is a major holiday, and work can stop for up to two weeks. A list of public holidays, including Lunar New Year, can be found on the Hong Kong government's Website.

Home electronics

A renovation is a good time to upgrade the electronics in your apartment. Your designer or contractor can add wiring for a computer network, telephone and home theater, cable television, home automation and alarm systems. Installing cable or empty conduit while the walls are being plastered and painted is less expensive than after completion.

Smoke and carbon monoxide detectors save lives and should be part of all renovations. Smoke detectors typically have a lifespan of 10 years, while new carbon monoxide detectors last seven years. See the detector's manual for testing and battery replacement instructions.

Kitchens

Most contractors in Hong Kong prefer not to supply kitchens. Instead, the contractor will install the surrounding infrastructure—lights, wiring and plumbing, as well as the floor, wall coverings and ceilings—and leave the rest to a specialist.

Kitchen specialists make efficient use of the space in Hong Kong's often-cramped homes.

Kitchen specialists use a "system" approach, where drawers, storage racks and countertops are sourced from a single manufacturer and installed as an integrated package. Many of these systems are from the United States or Europe, but a growing proportion of the materials are manufactured in China. The systems usually include built-in lighting; self-closing drawers with easy-to-clean plastic liners; storage units that make effective use of corners and other dead space; wipe-clean, laminated cupboard door panels; and molded countertops made from Corian™ and other synthetic materials.

Specialists add value by making efficient use of the space in Hong Kong's often-cramped kitchens. They ensure the kitchen has functional ergonomics, with adequate lighting and countertops of a workable height and depth. Specialists also understand the social role that kitchens play in many Western homes.

Kitchen specialists can supply and build around appliances, such as dishwashers, ovens, wine coolers and refrigerators. Get a second or third quote on these appliances, however, as kitchen specialists are not always the least expensive supplier.

In Hong Kong, kitchens must be protected by fire-resistant doors. To prevent the spread of fire, there are special engineering requirements for open kitchens.

Noise and neighbors

The Noise Control Ordinance (Cap. 400) states that construction work using powered equipment is prohibited between 19:00 and 07:00 and on general holidays, including Sundays, unless a valid construction noise permit is in force. Your building's deed of mutual covenant may also restrict the hours during which work can be carried out.

Before work starts, it can be a good idea to warn the neighbors immediately adjacent to your apartment. Minimizing renovation noise is also wise, especially during school examination season.

Paint

If you have children, spending a little extra on high-quality, washable paint can save you money over the long term. Ensure that surfaces are properly sealed and prepared before paint is applied, because even premium-quality paint will not adhere to flaking plaster or damp walls. Custom-tinted colors can be difficult to match when touch-ups are needed. Dark and bright colors will require multiple coats if you decide to repaint in a lighter, neutral shade. Mold-resistant paints are available for use in humid locations, such as bathrooms and kitchens.

Plumbing

In older apartments, you may need to update the drains and water pipes. Typically, this involves replacing all of the plumbing up to the point where your pipes connect to the building's water supply and drains. This will often result in a noticeable improvement in the flow of water, particularly if you are replacing unlined, galvanized steel pipes, which are prone to corrosion and have been banned since 1995.

Pipes are frequently embedded in walls and floors, so it makes sense to replace the electrical system, plumbing and flooring all at once.

Hong Kong apartments typically have one or more electric or gas-fueled water heaters. Central hot-water systems, like those found in North America, are rare.

Rainy season

Hong Kong's rainy season, which runs from May to September, is a poor time for renovations. In addition to typhoons that can demolish scaffolding and disrupt construction schedules, high humidity slows the curing of paint and plaster.

Salvage

Contractors usually assume anything removed from the property during the renovations belongs to them. If you want to keep or reuse materials, tell the contractor in advance.

Spare parts

When your project is finished, you will have surplus paint, flooring, tiles and other materials. Keep some of these scraps and note the name of the manufacturer, the brand name and the part or model numbers. There may be enough leftovers to make a repair later on. At the very least, the leftovers will make it easier for you to find matching replacement parts.

Tools

At a minimum, you'll need a flashlight, a conventional or an electronic tape measure, a digital camera and a way of taking notes and making sketches. A spirit level and a ball bearing or marble can help you spot floors and other elements that are not level. See the software entry in the "Information sources" chapter for suggested architecture, design and decoration programs.

What to renovate

If you are planning to sell your home in the short to medium term, focus on practical renovations like upgrading the plumbing, electrical system and windows. Avoid making changes that might discourage a potential buyer, like converting a bedroom into a spa. Use paint, wallpaper, light fixtures, furniture and artwork to personalize your home, rather than structural changes that may be out of fashion when you are ready to sell.

Where to buy

Even if you've hired a designer to manage your renovation, you owe it to yourself to visit Lockhart Road in Wanchai. Between Luard Road and Marsh Road, you'll find suppliers of virtually every kind of home decorating need, from doorknobs to bathtubs and from tiles to toilets. Trade shows organized by the Hong Kong Trade Development Council often feature building and decorating supplies and are another source of ideas and inspiration.

You can also buy supplies in China. There are malls throughout the country that sell all types of building materials, as well as cities and towns that specialize in manufacturing different products. In Guangdong, for example, Foshan is renowned for ceramics, while Guzhen focuses on lighting fixtures. The quality of these products ranges from superb (your iPhone, for instance, is assembled in Guangdong) to counterfeits that can pose a health and safety hazard to you and your family.

Contractors can have furniture and cabinetry custom-made in China and then shipped to Hong Kong for assembly and installation. I have had mixed results with these products. Kitchen and office cabinets with a plastic laminate finish have been durable and maintained their appearance over a decade of use. Some laminated wood cabinetry has also performed well, while painted wood cabinets have cracked and peeled. The manufacturer, materials and environment where the furniture is installed will all influence your satisfaction with the final results.

On Lockhart Road in Wanchai, you can find all kinds of building supplies.

You can also consider multinational suppliers such as Ikea and Bulthaup, which have English-language Websites and marketing materials.

Windows

If you are planning to replace your apartment's windows, installing double-glazed panels makes sense. Double-glazing is energy-efficient because the vacuum or inert gas between the windowpanes keeps the cool air inside your apartment and the hot air outdoors. Double-glazing also reduces the amount of outdoor noise transmitted into your apartment. If you have southern or western exposure, consider awnings or window film that reduces heat transmission.

According to the International Association of Certified Home Inspectors, aluminum windows should last 15–20 years, while wooden ones should last nearly 30 years. Double-glazed windows have a lifespan of 8–20 years.

In older apartments, your renovation may include replacing the existing windows with larger ones, but this can weaken the wall or change the appearance of the building. Obtain approval from the Buildings Department and your owners' corporation before starting work.

MONEY

Mortgages 153; Insurance 163; Taxes and Fees 167

MORTGAGES

A mortgage is a generic term for a loan secured by real property, such as land, a house or a condominium. A mortgage is also an encumbrance on the property, like an easement.

The basics

All mortgages include the following elements.

▲ A property that is being financed

▲ A mortgage document, which includes a promissory note stating the terms under which the borrower will repay the lender and a lien giving the lender an interest in the property

▲ A borrower, also known as a mortgagor

▲ A lender, also called a mortgagee

▲ Principal, which is the money borrowed by the mortgagor

▲ Interest, which the mortgagor pays to the lender for the use of the principal

▲ The right of foreclosure or repossession by the lender, if the borrower fails to observe the terms of the loan

▲ Completion, which is the date that the mortgage begins

▲ Redemption, which is the date that the mortgage ends, the date the interest and principal have been repaid to the lender and the date the lender's interest in the property ends

Lenders

See the Financing section of the "Information sources" chapter for a list of lenders.

Banks

Hong Kong's banks, which provide the majority of the city's mortgage loans, are overseen by the Hong Kong Monetary Authority (HKMA), a government body that reports to the Financial Secretary. Mortgages are big business in Hong Kong: in June 2015 there were more than $1 trillion in loans outstanding.

Brokers

Hong Kong has many mortgage brokers, who act as intermediaries between lenders and borrowers.

Nonbank lenders

A small but growing proportion of the city's mortgages is provided by Hong Kong's 1,300 nonbank lenders. These firms, which have historically focused on providing personal loans, are not regulated by the HKMA.

Nonbank lenders provide loans of up to 90% of a property's value, but charge significantly higher interest rates than banks.

Loan conditions

▲ The HKMA maintains a conservative lending environment. For example, under HKMA guidelines, in August 2015 the maximum loan-to-value (LTV) ratio was 60%. To qualify for a 60% LTV mortgage, the subject property would have to be residential, be valued at less than $10 million and the loan amount would be capped at $5 million. Furthermore, the home would have to be for the borrower's use (i.e., not a rental property), the borrower would have to earn the bulk of her income in Hong Kong and she could not have other outstanding mortgage loans. In contrast, the maximum LTV for a parking space purchased by a buyer earning the bulk of her income outside Hong Kong would be just 20%.[1]

▲ Current HKMA guidelines cap the tenor of new mortgage loans at 30 years, with loans for parking spaces limited to 15 years.

▲ HKMA guidelines limit a borrower's debt-to-income ratio to 50% of his total income per month for self-use properties and to 40% for non-self–use properties. Banks are expected to stress-test applicants' repayment ability based on a three percentage point increase in mortgage interest rates. Under the stress test, a borrower's debt-to-income ratio should not exceed 60% for self-use properties and 50% for non-self–use properties.

▲ Hong Kong mortgages are recourse loans. If you default and the lender forecloses, you are personally liable for the difference between the amount the lender recovers after disposing of the property and the outstanding balance of your mortgage.

▲ Mortgage loans normally require that the borrower take out fire insurance on the property.

▲ Bank policies often limit the sum of the building's age and the borrower's age to 60 or 70 years.

▲ Banks will lend to individuals, shell companies and operating companies.

▲ Fortnightly payment plans, which let you discharge your mortgage more quickly by making payments every two weeks rather than once a month, are available from many lenders.

▲ You will be charged a fee if you pay off your mortgage ahead of schedule. Lenders typically charge 3% of the outstanding balance if you redeem a mortgage within the first year, 2% in the second and 1% in the third. After three years, there is no prepayment penalty. Many lenders let you make penalty-free top-up payments.

▲ With some mortgages, the monthly payment remains constant regardless of changes in the interest rate. If the interest rate rises, the number of payments increases; if the interest rate falls, the number of payments decreases. With other mortgages, the amount of the monthly payment fluctuates with increases or decreases in interest rates, but the number of payments remains constant.

▲ Lenders often offer cash rebates, free property valuation services and other sweeteners as an incentive to borrow.

▲ Hong Kong lenders are conservative. There is often a large gap between the appraised value of a property and the actual purchase price.

Mortgage types

The following mortgages are available in Hong Kong.

Best lending rate

Hong Kong banks offer adjustable, prime rate–based loans, which are also called best lending rate loans. These are typically described as "prime minus X.X%." There isn't a single prime rate, and in August 2015, lenders used a prime rate of 5.0% or 5.25% with discounts ranging from 2.7% to 3.1%. In June 2015, loans in this category represented nearly 12% of new mortgages, with about two-thirds of borrowers paying a net annual interest rate (i.e., the prime rate less the discount) of 2.0%–2.5%.

Buy-to-let and commercial

Buy-to-let mortgages are designed for small landlords who purchase a home with the intention of renting it out. Buy-to-let mortgages are an alternative to conventional mortgages, which include a clause requiring that the owner or an immediate family member—not a tenant—occupy the dwelling. HKMA guidelines require lenders to apply a 30%–40% discount to rental income when calculating a borrower's ability to repay a loan.[2] For residential properties, the HKMA limits the LTV ratio to 30%–50%, depending on whether the borrower's income comes from Hong Kong or abroad and whether the borrower has mortgages on other properties. Similar limits apply to loans for offices, shops and industrial properties, where the LTV ratio can be as low as 20%.

Deposit-linked

With a deposit-linked mortgage, the bank pays the same interest rate on the balance of your bank account as it charges for the outstanding balance of your mortgage loan. For example, if your mortgage balance is $2 million and your bank account balance is $500,000, interest is only charged on $1.5 million.

Fixed-rate mortgages
In cooperation with participating banks, the government-owned Hong Kong Mortgage Corporation offers three- and five-year fixed-rate mortgages. In August 2015, interest rates for three-year mortgages ranged from 2.7% to 2.8%, while five-year rates were 3.3% to 3.4%.

Flexible
Flexible mortgages let borrowers underpay, take payment holidays, overpay and borrow against the mortgage without taking a second mortgage.

HIBOR
In June 2015, more than 85% of new mortgages were based on the Hong Kong interbank offered rate (HIBOR), which is the rate that banks use when lending each other money. HIBOR loans are typically based on the one-, three- or six-month interbank rate plus a fixed annual percentage. In August 2015, the fixed annual percentage ranged from 1.7% to 2.2%. Because they reflect changes in the international money markets, interest rates on HIBOR loans are more volatile than on prime rate–based loans. Some HIBOR loans limit the maximum interest rate payable to the lender's best lending rate.

Insured
The Hong Kong Mortgage Corporation and QBE Mortgage Insurance (Asia) offer insurance that lets banks provide higher LTV loans. The borrower pays the insurance premium, but the bank—not the borrower—is the beneficiary of the insurance policy.

With coverage from the Hong Kong Mortgage Corporation, the maximum LTV ratio is 90% for homes valued at less than $4 million; 90% or $3.6 million, whichever is lower, for homes valued between $4 million and $4.5 million; and 80% or $4.8 million, whichever is lower, for homes valued between $4.5 million and $6 million.

Reverse
The Hong Kong Mortgage Corporation operates a reverse mortgage program that lets homeowners over age 55 borrow money from participating banks against the equity in their homes. Under this program, the borrower continues to own the property and may live in it for the rest of his life. Borrowers can take out a reverse mortgage on

more than one property and receive monthly payouts either over a fixed term of 10, 15 or 20 years or throughout their lives. Homeowners may also borrow lump sums for specific purposes when needed.

Applying for a mortgage

Credit reports

When you apply for a mortgage, you will sign a document authorizing the lender to check your credit history. Hong Kong has one consumer credit reporting company, TransUnion (www.transunion.hk), which has records on 4.7 million consumers. Lenders typically combine their own research and credit-scoring methodology with information from TransUnion when approving or rejecting a mortgage application. The contents of your credit report can also influence the interest rate that the lender offers you. If you are buying through a company, the lender may request a report from Dun & Bradstreet (www.dnb.com.hk).

You can order a copy of your credit report from TransUnion's Website for a nominal fee. TransUnion's activities are regulated by the Code of Practice on Consumer Credit Data under the Personal Data (Privacy) Ordinance (Cap. 486).

Documents

Along with your mortgage application, you will need to give the bank:

▲ Your Hong Kong identity card or passport

▲ The preliminary sale and purchase agreement

▲ Proof of income, such as three months' salary deposit records in a bank passbook

▲ Your latest tax demand note or latest tax return

If the mortgage is in the name of a company, you will need to provide:

▲ Business registration certificate

▲ Certificate of incorporation

▲ Memorandum and articles of association

▲ Audited financial statements

▲ Bank statements

▲ Tax returns

Corporate borrowers may need to provide a personal guarantee from one or more of the shareholders as well as a board resolution authorizing the company to purchase the property.

Pre-approval

Hong Kong lenders will provide "approval in principle" or "indicative approval" for a mortgage in exchange for background information on you and your target property. This approval is not binding on the lender, but it does give you an idea of what mortgage products are available and how much you can borrow. You can also formally apply to the lender and get pre-approved for a mortgage. A pre-approved mortgage comes with a time limit and is binding on the lender.

Approval in principle and pre-approval give the buyer and the vendor confidence that the sale will be completed, and pre-approval can speed up the closing process.

The Hong Kong Mortgage Corporation offers a pre-approval service for its mortgage insurance.

Property survey

The lender will appoint a company to conduct a survey, which will document the property's legal description, location and condition. The lender will expect you to pay for the survey, although you can negotiate this point. Surveys typically cost about $3,000.

Success factors

Ultimately, the success or failure of your mortgage application will hinge on your income and debt load, the home's appraised value and the LTV ratio. However, there are things that you can do to improve your odds and, in some cases, get more attractive terms.

▲ Become a permanent resident. Meeting the government's permanent residency requirements tells the lender you are a person of good character and suggests that you plan on staying in Hong Kong.

▲ Exude stability. Banks like borrowers who have lived at the same address and worked for the same employer for a long time. Entrepreneurs and commissioned salespeople can be seen as poor risks because their incomes are more volatile than those of salaried employees.

▲ Get your paperwork in order. You'll save time and make it easier for the lender to approve your application if you have all of the documents they need.

▲ Be conventional. You are more likely to get a mortgage for a condominium than for a loft conversion or a farmhouse.

▲ Use introductions. A referral from your real estate agent, developer, employer, or a friend or neighbor can open doors that would otherwise remain shut.

▲ Make the numbers work. Ensure your LTV, debt-to-income ratio, mortgage amount and term are within the ranges specified by the bank and the HKMA's regulations. A large down payment also works in your favor.

▲ Leave some wiggle room. Add 7%–10% to the purchase price for closing costs and incidentals, and don't forget to budget for repairs and maintenance. Buying a little less than you can afford is sensible.

If your mortgage application is rejected, there are several things that you can do.

▲ Try another bank. Your application may have fallen afoul of the lender's internal policies. For example, they may have already filled their loan quota for a new development. Another lender may approve the same loan application.

▲ Reduce your principal. If the application is rejected because your income is too low, ask for a smaller loan.

▲ Fix your credit rating. If you haven't already done so, order a copy of your credit record from TransUnion and ensure that it is current and correct.

INSURANCE

Owning a property exposes you to a variety of risks, many of which can be managed with insurance.

When you buy insurance, you will deal with an agent who represents one insurance company. Or you can use a broker, who represents you and helps you find the best offering from a range of insurers. A knowledgeable broker can help you compare disparate policies and balance the sum insured against the deductible so that the coverage makes economic sense. They can also help you decipher the complex language used in many policies and ensure that the policy provides appropriate coverage.

All risk

All risk insurance covers all losses, except those that are specifically excluded in the policy. It is in contrast to named perils coverage, which applies only to losses from causes that are specifically listed in the policy. Because it is inclusive, all risk insurance is usually expensive.

Domestic helper

If you employ a domestic helper, you are legally required to insure her against injury and death.

Fire

Fire insurance covers the structure—but not the contents—of a home against damage caused by fire. It can also cover losses due to earthquakes, storms, burst pipes, landslides, subsidence and similar risks, either as part of the policy or under a separate rider.

You need fire insurance to obtain a mortgage, and lenders often arrange this with the mortgage. If you live in a condominium, the building's master policy may provide sufficient fire insurance coverage to satisfy your mortgage lender. The lender will ask for proof of coverage, which can be provided by your owners' corporation.

In Hong Kong, the beneficial interest in a property passes to you as soon as you sign a binding agreement to purchase the property. As a result, you should take out insurance as soon as you sign the agreement, even if you will not take possession for several months.

Flood

Flood insurance covers overland flooding, which occurs when water enters a dwelling after a river, stream or lake overflows and covers normally dry land. Burst pipes and overflowing sewers are typically covered by fire insurance, not flood insurance.

Homeowners

Homeowners insurance is a package policy that covers damage to the structure of the home, the contents of the home, the cost of temporary accommodation if the home is damaged or destroyed and personal liability insurance. Tenants insurance is similar to homeowners insurance, but does not cover the structure of the building.

Homeowners insurance usually excludes illegal structures, and lapses if the home is unoccupied for 30–60 days. Some plans offer 10%–50% additional coverage during the summer months, when typhoons and heavy rains are common.[1]

Landlord

Landlord insurance protects owners from damage caused by tenants, including theft and vandalism. Typically, landlord insurance covers public liability, damage from burst pipes and lost rental revenue due to fires, storms and other risks. Some policies include legal and travel expenses and cover furniture and other effects that the landlord provides to tenants.

Mortgage

See the "Mortgages" chapter for information about mortage insurance.

Professional liability

Professional liability insurance is bought by people and companies that provide specialist services to protect them from negligence lawsuits. It is also known as professional indemnity and errors and omissions insurance.

If you suffer a loss because a supplier made a mistake—for example, the plans provided by an architect were defective and your home collapsed—professional liability insurance increases the likelihood that you could sue the architect and successfully collect damages.

In 2012, the Estate Agents Authority, the statutory body that regulates real estate agents in Hong Kong, published a best practices checklist. The checklist recommends that agents carry professional liability insurance and that clients' money is covered by insurance. However, this is only a recommendation, and there is no mention of insurance in the Estate Agents Ordinance (Cap. 511).

Public liability

Public liability insurance covers claims from damage to property and bodily injury, except those arising from the ownership of automobiles and aircraft. Public liability insurance is usually included in a homeowners policy, but this may not provide sufficient coverage for a renovation project, particularly if the job includes work at height on the outside of a building, like installing air conditioners. Ask to see proof of insurance from the contractor and obtain additional coverage from your insurance agent, if necessary.

Title

Title insurance protects a buyer if there is a defect in a property's title, like a lien, that was not discovered when he purchased the property. In Hong Kong, title insurance is not usually purchased by individual homeowners. Title insurance is used in large commercial transactions, such as the formation of real estate investment trusts.

Workers' compensation

You can be held responsible for injuries that people sustain in your home, including construction workers. Normally, workers' compensation insurance is provided by the company that employs the workers. However, some contractors will charge separately for coverage, especially if the contractor employs subcontractors and self-employed tradespeople.

Like public liability cases, workers' compensation claims can become a problem for the homeowner if the claim amount exceeds the contractor's ability to pay.

TAXES AND FEES

The Hong Kong government charges taxes and fees on the acquisition, occupancy, conversion, lease and disposal of real estate. Hong Kong's developers, investors and lawyers are skilled at finding and exploiting loopholes to avoid paying these costs, which can add millions of dollars to the price of a home.

Some tax-reduction techniques—for example, selling the holding company that owns a home rather than the home itself to avoid paying stamp duty—are well established. Others, such as using industrial property for residential purposes, are illegal but tolerated. Still others, like Cheung Kong's sale of individual rooms in the Apex Horizon Hotel in 2013, test the boundaries. Cheung Kong ultimately reached an agreement with the Securities and Futures Commission (SFC) to "unwind" the sale of 360 hotel rooms and refund the buyers' money with interest and legal fees after the SFC ruled that the sale constituted an offer to participate in a collective investment scheme under the Securities and Futures Ordinance (Cap. 571).[1]

Transactions that are structured to minimize taxes usually carry additional expenses, such as legal and audit fees. They can also expose you to unexpected liabilities and risks.

Government rent

Under the Government Rent (Assessment and Collection) Ordinance (Cap. 515), properties in the New Territories, properties north of Boundary Street in Kowloon, properties with land leases granted on or after May 27, 1985, and properties with nonrenewable land leases that were extended on or after May 27, 1985, must pay government rent, which is fixed at 3% of the property's ratable value (see the Rates section, below). The rent payable is recorded by the Land Registry and appears on the land search printout that is provided by the real estate agent.

Government rent is payable by the property owner and there are exemptions for indigenous villagers. Failure to pay government rent, even if the rent is for a period before the current owner purchased the property, is a breach of the land lease, which enables the government to re-enter the property.

The Rating and Valuation Department publishes an explanatory booklet, Your Rates and Government Rent, which is available free of charge on the department's Website.[2]

Income and capital gains taxes

Hong Kong does not have a capital gains tax. However, if you buy and sell large numbers of properties, the Inland Revenue Department can classify your activities as a business that must file a tax return and pay profits tax.[3] You will also need a business license and an annual audit of your company accounts.

Interest on a residential mortgage is deductible from your net assessable income under salaries tax or from your total income under a personal assessment. Since 2008–09, the deduction has been capped at $100,000 per year.[4]

Lease modification and conversion premiums

When land is converted from a low-value use, such as agriculture, to a more profitable application, like commercial or residential, the developer pays the government a premium reflecting the increase in the property's value. Developers also pay a premium when a lease is modified to allow the conversion of a low-rise building into a high-rise complex or an industrial building into an apartment.

Individuals who buy an apartment under the Home Ownership Scheme or another subsidized housing program must pay the government a premium before they sell, rent or assign their homes on the open market.[5]

Rates

Rates are a property tax levied by the government under the Rating Ordinance (Cap. 116). Rates are paid quarterly and are calculated as a percentage of the annual rental revenue that a property would generate if it was vacant and available for rent. The Rating Ordinance includes both a mechanism for owners and occupiers to contest a property's ratable value and an appeal process. In the 2014–15 financial year, rates were charged at 5% of the rental yield.

Both the owner and the occupier of a property are liable for rates. In practice, the person who pays is determined by the terms of the lease agreement between the owner and occupier. If there is no agreement to the contrary, the occupier is liable for rates.

Stamp duty

Under the Stamp Duty Ordinance (Cap. 117), Hong Kong collects stamp duty on property purchases, lease agreements and other transactions. Exemptions are available when property is sold through a court order, when property is sold to the government, when the transaction involves a close family member or the disposal of a deceased person's estate and under other circumstances. Stamp duty is payable within 30 days of the transaction date.[6]

Ad valorem stamp duty
There are two scales for ad valorem stamp duty in Hong Kong. Scale 2 applies to residential property acquired by a Hong Kong permanent

Scale 1		
From	To	Rate
$1	$2,000,000	1.5%
$2,000,000	$2,176,470	$30,000 + 20% of excess over $2m
$2,176,470	$3,000,000	3%
$3,000,000	$3,290,330	$90,000 + 20% of excess over $3m
$3,290,330	$4,000,000	4.5%
$4,000,000	$4,428,580	$180,000 + 20% of excess over $4m
$4,428,580	$6,000,000	6%
$6,000,000	$6,720,000	$360,000 + 20% of excess over $6m
$6,720,000	$20,000,000	7.5%
$20,000,000	$21,739,130	$1.5m + 20% of excess over $20m
$21,739,130	∞	8.5%

resident who does not own other residential property in Hong Kong at the time of acquisition. Scale 1, which took effect on February 23, 2013, applies to all other cases.

Scale 2		
From	To	Rate
$1	$2,000,000	$100
$2,000,000	$2,351,760	$100 + 10% of excess over $2m
$2,351,760	$3,000,000	1.5%
$3,000,000	$3,290,320	$45,000 + 10% of excess over $3m
$3,290,320	$4,000,000	2.25%
$4,000,000	$4,428,570	$90,000 + 10% of excess over $4m
$4,428,570	$6,000,000	3%
$6,000,000	$6,720,000	$180,000 + 10% of excess over $6m
$6,720,000	$20,000,000	3.75%
$20,000,000	$21,739,120	$750,000 + 10% of excess over $20m
$21,739,120	∞	4.25%

Buyer's stamp duty
Effective October 27, 2012, the government introduced a buyer's stamp duty on the purchase of Hong Kong residential property by any person, including local and foreign companies, other than a Hong Kong permanent resident. The duty is 15% of the purchase price and is charged on top of the ad valorem stamp duty and the special stamp duty, if applicable.[7]

Leases
Stamp duty is charged on lease contracts at the following rates. For leases, stamp duty is usually split between the tenant and the landlord.

Lease period	Rate
Undefined	0.25% of the yearly or average yearly rent
Under 1 year	0.25% of the total rent payable over the lease term
1–3 years	0.5% of the yearly or average yearly rent
Over 3 years	1% of the yearly or average yearly rent

Special stamp duty

To discourage speculators, the government introduced a special stamp duty that applies to residential property that is acquired by an individual or a company after October 27, 2012, and sold within three years of the purchase date.

Holding period	Rate
6 months or less	20%
6–12 months	15%
12–36 months	10%

CASE STUDIES

CASE STUDIES

AN APARTMENT IN POKFULAM

Property

A four-bedroom, 2,200-square-foot (177 square meter) apartment in a 15-story building in Pokfulam. Built in 1975, the home includes a maid's room, a balcony and parking.

Time line

The preliminary sale and purchase agreement was signed on October 14, 2004. The sale was completed on December 9, 2004. We moved in on February 28, 2005.

Condition

The apartment's fixtures, fittings and decoration were mostly original. The windows had a mixture of iron and aluminum frames. The electrical system included old (BS 546 standard) and new three-blade (BS 1363) outlets and an ancient circuit breaker panel. Water pipes had been mounted on the walls in one bathroom. The kitchen counters and cupboards were ready to collapse. The kitchen and both bathrooms were covered in garish ceramic tiles.

As is common in Pokfulam, the building is near several cemeteries. There was a statutory order for repair work to be carried out on the slope behind the complex. However, as the order had been registered several years before we purchased the apartment, we negotiated to have the vendor deposit money with his solicitors to cover the cost of repairs.

Despite these drawbacks, the apartment was in our price range. It was bright and airy, had a high efficiency ratio (the ratio of gross to usable floor area) and included a sea view. The poor condition of the interior was an advantage, because it meant we wouldn't have to pay for and then replace someone else's decorations. The complex is close to schools and public transport and has a swimming pool, tennis courts

Before: The kitchen counters and cupboards were disintegrating and a range hood had been installed as an afterthought. The linoleum tile floor was cracked and dirty.

After: A system kitchen, a new tile floor and an aluminum ceiling with recessed lights make all the difference. Built-in storage and space for a microwave oven and wine cooler were added in the pantry at the back of the kitchen.

and a grocery store. Few buildings in the neighborhood matched this combination of location, space and affordability.

Apartment purchase

Item	Amount
Purchase price	$11,000,000
Real estate agent's commission	110,000
Stamp duty	412,710
Renovations	1,040,000
Legal fees, including disbursements	8,950
Major appliances	50,612
Total	$12,622,272

Renovations

We interviewed three contractors and picked one who had recently completed a major renovation in a similar apartment for one of our friends. The contractor's English was good, he was personable and he produced computer-aided design drawings as well as elaborate renderings of the finished rooms in the apartment. Most important, he had satisfied our friend, whose project included a gourmet kitchen, a fireplace and several other unusual design elements. Our friend was extremely particular about his apartment's design, construction and material, so we believed we were in good hands.

After consulting the contractor, we determined that all of the wiring and plumbing needed to be replaced. We wanted split-type, reverse-cycle air conditioners; double-glazed windows throughout the apartment; built-in storage in the pantry and each of the bedrooms; an entertainment center in the living room; plenty of electrical, telephone and cable TV outlets; and solid wood floors.

To maintain a sense of space, we picked a light-colored hardwood floor from South America, which was used everywhere except in the bathrooms, the kitchen and pantry and the maid's room.

Maximizing the space in the apartment's galley-style kitchen was a priority. We bought a high-quality system kitchen—complete with cupboards, built-in lighting, racks, Corian™ countertops and integrated sinks—from a specialty supplier. The kitchen supplier also sold us a futuristic range hood that, while attractive, broke down twice shortly after the warranty expired. We also purchased a drawer-style dishwasher, a large refrigerator/freezer and a full-sized gas oven from appliance vendors, rather than the kitchen contractor or gas company. Medium-sized, off-white ceramic tiles covered the walls of the kitchen and all but one wall in the common bathroom. Blue, textured tiles were installed on the kitchen floor and the remaining wall in the common bathroom. A white, aluminum drop-ceiling, with recessed halogen and fluorescent lighting was installed in the kitchen and in both bathrooms.

The sanitary ware was replaced in both bathrooms. We installed an electronically controlled, gas-fueled water heater, and replaced the tub in the en suite bathroom in the master bedroom with a large, tiled shower enclosure, complete with a bench, a window overlooking the nearby hillside and a rain-shower–style showerhead. Heat lamps were installed in both bathrooms to take the edge off cool winter mornings.

The balcony was also refurbished. We installed new tiles on the floor and one wall, re-plastered the ceiling and replaced two walls with glass panels. The original sliding balcony doors were replaced with a folding door with double-glazed panels. See the "Approvals and permits" chapter for more information on the balcony.

On Monday morning, the workers arrived. Within 48 hours, the apartment was reduced to bare cement, with holes where the pipes and wires once were. As the workers stripped the apartment, we met the contractor in Wanchai, where we spent the first of several mornings in building supply showrooms, choosing tile, toilets and sinks, taps and the other hardware for our new home.

Despite the Christmas and New Year holidays, the contractor handed over the apartment on schedule. This allowed us to move in and get settled during the Lunar New Year holidays.

Before: The bathroom in the master bedroom featured ugly pink and blue ceramic tiles, surface-mounted plumbing and an old-style water heater.

After: The common bathroom with new tiles, an extractor fan, drop-ceiling and sanitary ware. The electronically controlled, gas-fueled water heater is shown at the top left.

Two days into the renovation, the parquet floor in the dining room had been removed and the kitchen was reduced to bare walls.

Midway through the project, new tiles had been installed on the kitchen walls and the rough plastering was finished.

Problems

Three aspects of the renovation proved troublesome: the balcony, floors and glazing.

Balcony
When the contractor retiled the balcony, he neglected to replace the tile on a four-inch strip outside the front balcony wall, an omission that wasn't noticed until the scaffolding was removed. To fix this oversight, the scaffold was reinstalled and a new insurance policy taken out, as the original policy had lapsed.

Floors
While the tile floors in the bathrooms and kitchen were level, the timber floors undulated and several sections had cracked or chipped planks. As the flooring used tongue-and-groove construction, single planks could not be replaced.

Glazing
Several of the double-glazed panels had scratches. When the contractor declined to replace them, a closer inspection revealed that more than three-quarters of the glass panels in the apartment had scratches, bubbles or flaws in the sealing. The glass in the shower stall door and in the balcony panels had similar problems, all of which the contractor claimed were normal.

Ultimately, the contractor refused to replace the defective glass or floors. With the help of a solicitor, I negotiated a partial payment on his final invoice.

Lessons learned

With large budgets come great expectations. If we had done a minor renovation (or been renting the apartment), we would have overlooked the unfinished balcony tiles. But with a million-dollar renovation bill, we were determined to get everything just right.

The building's age added several quirks to the renovation. For example, several walls were noticeably out of plumb. The exterior walls included cutouts and shelves for window-type air conditioners, both of which had to be retained to comply with the building's deed of mutual covenant. In the end, windows with interior louvers were installed in the cutouts.

At the start of the renovation, we had hoped to save money by re-surfacing the existing hardwood parquet floors. However this proved impractical, given the condition of the wood.

Renovation

Item	Amount
Plumbing	$44,000
Electrical	83,000
Hardwood flooring*	77,000
Ceramic tile*	107,000
Sanitary ware	37,500
Air-conditioning*	58,500
Glazing and aluminum ceilings	123,000
Kitchen sinks, cupboards and counters	73,000
Paint	73,000
Closets and entertainment center	142,000
Carpentry and masonry	112,000
Design fee	39,000
Demolition and clean-up	71,000
Total	$1,040,000

* Includes installation

The built-in entertainment unit, which was designed to house our music collection, sound system, TV and knickknacks, proved to be a disappointment. As with the bedroom closets, the contractor had sub-assemblies for the entertainment unit fabricated in China and then assembled them in our apartment. But after about eight months, the wood began to shrink, showing nailheads and other defects. While this wasn't catastrophic, it did detract from the overall impression.

Our original plans for the living room called for a false ceiling with recessed lighting and housings to hide the split-type air conditioners. The cost of these features outweighed their utility and we canceled them.

Finally, we used less expensive matte latex paint for several rooms. That proved to be false economy, as the more expensive semi-gloss paint we used elsewhere in the apartment was more durable and easier to clean.

A decade of experience

After living with the home and the renovations for 10 years, we learned several additional lessons.

Air conditioners

After being repaired several times, the split-type air conditioners have been replaced. The air conditioners we installed in 2005 use a refrigerant that has since been banned. As a result, when we replaced the compressors and head units, we also had to replace the connecting pipes that were buried in apartment walls.

Appliances

As the major appliances—including the dishwasher and the clothes washer and dryer failed, we replaced them with Miele products. While Miele is expensive, it is durable. At one point, we were told that the sole supplier of the water filters used in our refrigerator was going to stop making them. The manufacturer relented, but the price of the filter cartridges has risen from $450 to $730.

Built-in furniture

The entertainment center, bathroom vanity cabinets and some of the bedroom closets have not aged well. The shrinkage mentioned above continued, and some of the finishes have delaminated. One of the entertainment center's main functions was to house our collection of CDs and DVDs, which have since been removed from their jewel cases and stored in large wallets, leaving empty shelves behind.

The finish on the doors of the bathroom vanity cabinet has cracked and de-laminated.

Flooring
A broken flush water valve in the common bathroom flooded all four bedrooms and part of the hallway. Shortly after the water was cleaned up, the timber began to swell and warp, and more than half of the flooring had to be replaced. We obtained a close—but not perfect—match for the timber.

Glazing
The seals on several large, double-glazed panels have failed and need to be replaced. This is within the expected lifespan of these products.

Kitchen cabinets
In contrast with the other cabinetry, the laminated plastic cabinets in the kitchen have performed well and look good. We have had some difficulty getting a replacement handle for one cabinet.

Lighting and electrical
In future renovations, I would put the heat lamps on timers, so they could not be left on unnecessarily. We had difficulty finding replacement glass globes for the ceiling lights in the bedrooms, and a broken plastic diffuser on an under-cabinet light in the kitchen meant

that the entire fixture had to be replaced. That was both annoying and wasteful. We have been experimenting with light-emitting diode (LED) lights and are happy with their efficiency and low heat output. I would install LED-based nightlights under the vanity cabinets in the bathrooms. I would also bury empty conduit in the walls between the rooms to facilitate the installation of computer, and home security and entertainment systems.

A FACTORY
IN WONG CHUK HANG

Property

A 3,500-square-foot (gross) (325 square meter) unit in a 15-story flatted factory building that was completed in 1975. The building is in Wong Chuk Hang, a Hong Kong Island neighborhood that was popular with manufacturers.

Time line

A preliminary sale and purchase agreement for the purchase of the factory was signed on April 19, 2005. The transaction was completed on May 30, and we moved in on June 30, 2005.

A preliminary sale and purchase agreement for the sale of the factory was signed on August 3, 2010. The sale was completed on October 19, 2010.

A complicated purchase

On weekends, my family would often drive to Shek O and other destinations on the south side of Hong Kong Island. That trip would take us through Wong Chuk Hang, a series of factory buildings sandwiched between working-class Aberdeen and Shouson Hill, which is one of Hong Kong's most exclusive neighborhoods.

On these trips, I noticed how out of place the factories were in Hong Kong's new, service-based economy. It was common knowledge that Hong Kong's industrial base was moving to southern China, and I wondered if these buildings might offer an investment opportunity.

I began researching Wong Chuk Hang and learned that the neighborhood had attracted interest from several large developers, who had received approval to erect hotels. Wong Chuk Hang Estate, a 1960s-era public housing project that was once home to nearly 15,000 people,

Before: The factory was dirty and filled with debris. Many windows were broken and there were no lights or electrical outlets.

After: The front of the factory became a daylight studio, with new lights, windows, air conditioning and paint. The floor was later refinished with medium-gray epoxy paint.

was being redeveloped. Ocean Park, a nearby amusement park, was starting a US$700 million redevelopment project that included two new hotels. Finally, there were rumors that the Mass Transit Railway (MTR) would build a line through the neighborhood.

After wandering around the area, I found a suitable unit, which was listed for $1.6 million. I made a verbal offer, which was accepted. After a few days, the agent told me there was a "problem," and the vendor had backed out of the sale. A week later, the problem had been solved and the unit was back on the market. But now there was a new vendor, a confirmor who had bought the property to resell without taking possession. I could still buy the unit, but the price was now $260,000 higher. Despite feeling like I had been ripped off, I paid cash for the property.

Condition

The factory's last tenant, a steam laundry, had departed some months earlier. Several windows were broken or missing, and garbage and scrap were strewn everywhere. The laundry equipment and internal partitions had been removed, leaving an area where a boiler had once stood that was black with soot. The back of the unit was dark, but the front had large windows and southern exposure.

The building was reasonably quiet. Many units were either empty or used as warehouses. And while the building's aesthetics were rough, I was encouraged to see that structural repairs were being carried out on the loading dock at the back of the building.

Renovations

To get the process started, I began researching loft conversions, which were the closest thing to what I was attempting. I found little information on local lofts, but I was able to buy several books about projects in the United States and Europe. These books provided inspiration and helped convey my design ideas to the contractor.

I had planned to keep the floor in its original condition—patched, cracked and discolored—but with a clear coat of epoxy. The initial results looked good, but within two days the epoxy grew opaque in places. After considerable experimentation, the contractor found a medium-gray shade of epoxy that didn't fog up and looked good.

Replacing the windows was a priority. Many were broken or painted-over, and one set had been replaced with sliding patio doors that were used to remove equipment. Leaks are a common problem in Hong Kong, and even after the windows were replaced, puddles of water would appear after heavy rains.

Before departing, the previous owner had stripped the electrical system all the way back to the main circuit breaker, which meant that I needed to install new lighting as well as power outlets. As I had planned an industrial look for the space, I asked the contractor to surface-mount the electrical conduit along with cable for the telephone and a local area network for the computer system. The contractor also installed fluorescent work lights and halogen spotlights. I paid close attention to ensuring that the electrical system was properly installed and tested.

One of the attractions of a loft—its open space—is also a drawback in Hong Kong's climate, where air-conditioning is essential for 10 months of the year. I solved this problem by installing a brick wall to divide the space in two, so the blackout studio was only cooled when it was in use. I installed four split-type air conditioners, two in each studio, and painted all of the interior walls flat white. Later, I built a small storage room in one corner of the daylight studio, next to an exterior wall that faced a noisy factory in an adjacent building. In addition to giving me a place to store files and supplies, the room provided acoustic isolation when the factory was operating.

Borrowing an idea from a design book, I found a local sailmaker to manufacture room dividers out of synthetic sailcloth. They stitched pockets into the top and bottom of the dividers, through which I ran stainless steel pipe. The dividers were then suspended between the ceiling and floor on steel cables and turnbuckles. Sailcloth is ideal for this application because it is strong, translucent, lightweight and allows air to flow around it.

Before: Despite the mess, the factory's high ceilings and natural light had potential.

After: A bright, spacious client lounge in the daylight studio.

Plumbing was a slightly more complex issue. Previously, the unit had separate bathrooms for men and women, one of which was converted into a storeroom. I turned the storeroom back into a bathroom with a shower and a sink, and added a kitchenette outside. This allowed me to minimize costs by concentrating the plumbing, tile work and drop-ceilings into one area.

A studio is born

I liked the idea of having a New York-style loft as an office. But Hong Kong's zoning regulations draw a clear (if often ignored) distinction between commercial and industrial use, and the building was designated as industrial.

I considered using the factory as a self-storage facility, but rejected this idea. The cost of staff, advertising, security, etc., only made sense with a much larger unit than I was comfortable buying.

In my research, I learned that in 2004, the government had published a revised outline zoning plan for the area that included an expanded range of approved applications. The zoning plan included a category that was close to my business: "Office (audio visual recording studio, design and media production, office related to industrial use only)."

That inspired me to build a rental studio for professional photographers. There were a few such facilities in Hong Kong, but most were in Chai Wan, an industrial area that is distant from the central business district. The studios were run by professional photographers who rented them out as a sideline. From discussions with industry contacts, I learned that one photographer would use another's studio, but this often resulted in an unsatisfactory lack of privacy. I also discovered that many studios were cramped and unpleasant places to work.

I studied the Websites of studios in other cities and decided that my space would be independent; there would be no one looking over your shoulder while you worked. I created a Website that included everything from ceiling heights and the dimensions of our freight elevators to floor plans and public transit information. I offered Wi-Fi; free coffee, tea and soft drinks; a sound system; and other amenities to make the studio pleasant and productive. I even recruited a five-star hotel to be our official caterer.

I installed makeup stations, hair salon chairs, a selection of background paper and a large chroma key screen for video shoots. I considered spending $75,000–$100,000 on a professional cyclorama, but decided to wait until I had a better sense of market demand. After adding a pipe grid in the ceiling, where lights and props could be suspended, the studio was operational.

The studio was a modest success, attracting local and international photographers, video production companies, advertising agencies and even a TV network. The space was used for ad campaigns, catalogs, magazine articles and fashion shoots. It was also rented out for an exhibition of video projectors, photographer training, bagpipe practice and the occasional party. In addition to providing a source of passive income, it kept me in touch with Hong Kong's creative community. Five years after the studio closed, I continue to receive rental inquiries.

Factory purchase

Item	Amount
Purchase price	$1,880,000
Real estate agent's commission	18,800
Stamp duty	14,100
Initial renovations*	292,256
Legal fees, including disbursements	6,500
Total	$2,211,656

*Includes wiring and lights, air conditioners, water heater, sanitary ware, windows, internal walls and painting and decorating.

Industrial experience

Working in an industrial building for five years was educational. One issue was a lack of restaurants, other than a few canteens serving the remaining manufacturers in the area. I joined the Aberdeen Boat Club to have a place to park, eat lunch and meet clients for a drink.

Before: The laundry's boiler sat in this corner of what became the blackout studio.

After: A brick wall separates the daylight studio at the front of the factory from the blackout studio.

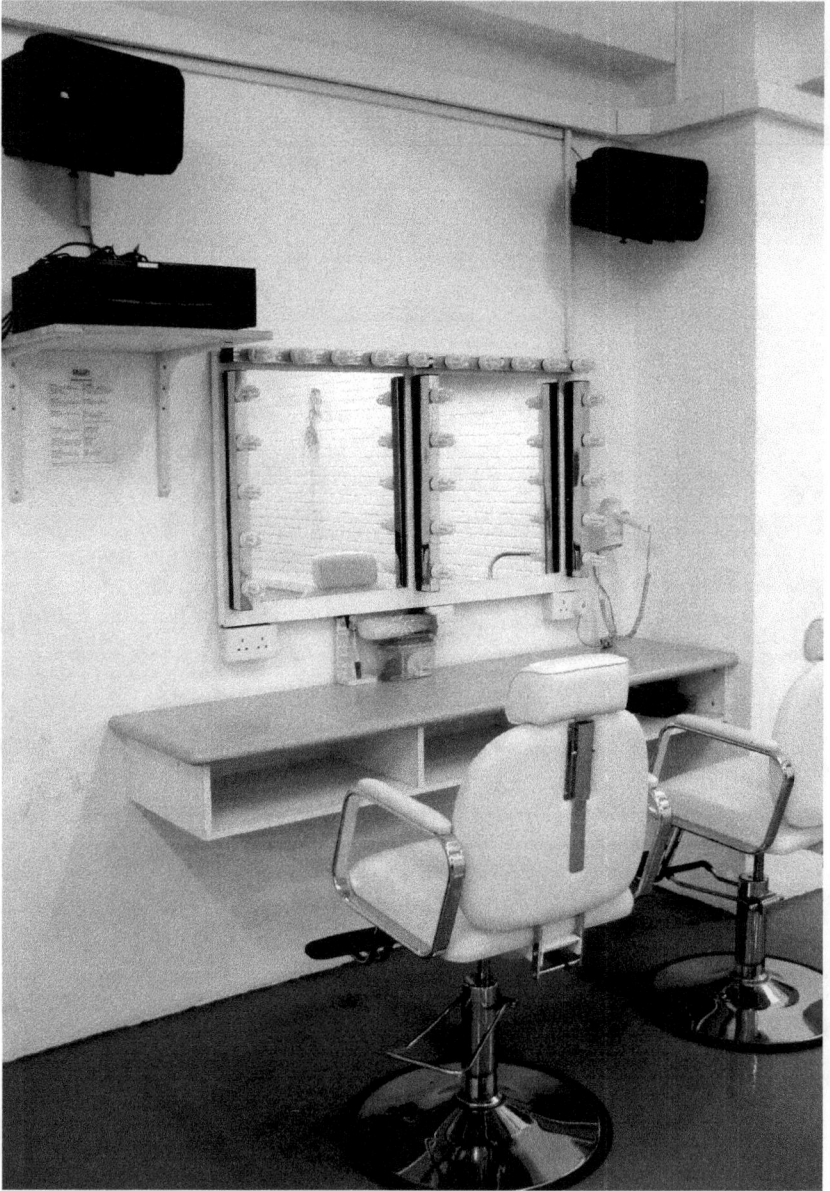

Makeup stations and the sound system in the blackout studio.

The daylight studio with a sailcloth divider.

Despite being only 30 years old, the building was in poor condition. In addition to leaks during rainstorms, the interior concrete walls suffered from spalling. The freight and passenger elevators had passed the point of repair and needed to be replaced. We also experienced a flood in the blackout studio when a standpipe broke.

At one point, the owners' committee passed a resolution to start a renovation program that would cover essential repairs. The plans were approved and the committee began collecting money, with my share coming to $140,000. After months of meetings and heated negotiations, the renovations were shelved because some owners refused to pay. Deposits were returned to those who cooperated and the building continued to deteriorate.

I shared a floor with a company that made a traditional Chinese medicine that included peppermint. But not all of my neighbors were equally pleasant. Toward the end of my stay, a meat wholesaler rented one of the building's upper floors. Each morning, their staff would load trucks with frozen chicken, beef and fish, which would be delivered to restaurants throughout the city. In the afternoons, the company would receive 45-foot containers of meat from Canada, Brazil and the United States. Pallets of frozen meat would often be left in the elevators, where they would slowly melt, leaving puddles of blood on the floor, much to the delight of the cockroaches.

In December 2007, the government approved the construction of the MTR's South Island Line (East), which will run from South Horizons to Admiralty, with a depot in Wong Chuk Hang. The announcement of the new train line produced an immediate spike in the price of property in Wong Chuk Hang. As details of the project were revealed, it became clear that the neighborhood would be a major construction site for at least five years. Worse, my sunny southern view, which included hundreds of egrets, would soon be replaced by a concrete railway trestle.

At that point, I decided to sell the unit rather than endure several years of noise and disruption. Considering the proceeds from the sale, the rental income from the studio and having a home for my business for five years, owning the factory was a positive experience.

Factory sale

Item	Amount
Sale price	$10,250,000
Real estate agent's commission	($25,625)
Legal fees, including disbursements	($11,857)
Sale proceeds	**$10,212,518**
Less purchase price	($2,211,656)
Gross profit	**$8,000,862**

AN OFFICE IN SAI YING PUN

Property

A 707-square-foot (66 square meter) office in Singga Commercial Center (SCC). Built in 1983, SCC is a 41-story, Grade B tower in Sai Ying Pun, on the west side of Hong Kong Island.

Time line

A preliminary sale and purchase agreement to buy the office was signed on January 20, 2011. The purchase was completed on March 4.

A preliminary sale and purchase agreement to sell the office was signed on October 24. The sale was completed on December 9, 2011.

The purchase

After selling the flatted factory in August 2010, I decided to rent an office in SCC. Where the factory had a private bathroom, individual air-conditioning and high ceilings, SCC had shared bathrooms, central air-conditioning and ceilings that I could reach up and touch. Furthermore, the bathrooms needed renovation and the central air-conditioning struggled to keep up with high temperatures during the summer months.

Offices in SCC come in two sizes: end units that are 1,186 square feet (gross) and middle units that are 707 square feet. I rented a larger unit, and despite SCC's shortcomings, I came to like the building and its unobstructed harbor views. SCC was one minibus ride and a short walk from my home.

At the end of 2010, I decided to buy an office in SCC. Through an agent, I found a 707-square-foot unit on a middle floor for $3.9 million. The office had carpet, a drop ceiling, some built-in storage and a glass-paneled manager's office.

The office also had a tenant, a small trading company that was paying below-market rent. The company's lease was scheduled to end in the fall of 2011.

Office purchase

Item	Amount
Purchase price	$3,888,500
Real estate agent's commission	$38,885
Stamp duty	$87,413
Legal fees, including disbursements	$8,200
Total	$4,022,998

The office had a glass-paneled manager's office and some built-in storage.

The sale

As I waited for the tenant's lease to expire, I worked with an interior designer to create a preliminary plan for the office. I also received a steady stream of phone calls from real estate agents asking if I wanted to sell the office. In response, I quoted a high asking price that I did not expect to get.

On October 20, 2011, while I was in Shanghai researching *Landed China*, my assistant, Rickie, called. An agent had appeared at the office with a deposit check and a signed offer that met my asking price. What should she do? I told Rickie to take the check, and four days later I signed a provisional sale and purchase agreement.

Office sale

Item	Amount
Sale price	$5,302,500
Real estate agent's commission	($53,025)
Legal fees, including disbursements	($7,500)
Sale proceeds	**$5,241,975**
Rent from tenant*	$44,376
Less purchase price	($4,022,998)
Gross profit	HK$1,263,353

*Net of management fees. The Hong Kong government did not charge rates during this period.

Singga Commercial Center offers excellent views of Victoria Harbor.

Lessons learned

With one exception, the purchase and the sale of the office went smoothly. The exception was the tenant's lease, which had a two-year term. When I read the lease, however, I noticed that the start and end dates were 23 months apart, something my lawyer failed to catch. In the end, the tenant stayed for the full 24 months.

The value of the office benefited from a general upward trend in the property market. An extension to the Mass Transit Railway's Island Line also helped the price. The extension was announced in October 2007, work began in July 2009 and Sai Ying Pun Station opened in March 2015.

RESOURCES

Property Buyer's Checklist

Information Sources

PROPERTY BUYER'S CHECKLIST

Buildings and land

▲ Does the **building** have a reputation for quality issues, such as falling glass panels or other problems?

▲ Are the **common areas** clean and well maintained? Do they need to be overhauled?

▲ Are there **dangerous slopes** on the property? Are the property owners responsible for dangerous slopes on an adjacent property?

▲ Has a **death,** suicide or violent crime occurred in the home?

▲ Are there any **easements** or rights of way on the property?

▲ What **facilities**—e.g., a gym, swimming pool or tennis court—are included in the complex? Are the facilities open, clean and well maintained? Are they available to all residents?

▲ Are there any hidden **fees** for parking, facilities, ground rent, etc.?

▲ Does the home have bad *feng shui* or an inauspicious address?

▲ How much are the **management fees**?

▲ Is the building mainly populated by **owner-occupiers** or tenants?

▲ Is a **parking** space included? How much are the management fees and rates (property taxes) for the parking space? Is guest parking available?

▲ How much are the **rates**?

▲ Are there any problematic **regulations**, such as restrictions on pets, in the house rules or deed of mutual covenant?

▲ Are major **renovations** and special assessments planned?

▲ Is the area affected by **subsidence?**

▲ Has a land **survey** been conducted?

▲ Does the property include **universal design** features that would make it suitable for elderly or disabled people?

▲ Does the unit have any **unusual liabilities**, like maintenance of a roof?

▲ Are there many rental **vacancies** or units for sale in the building?

▲ Does the building comply with **zoning** regulations?

Developers and off the plan purchases

▲ How long has the developer been in **business**?

▲ Does the developer have a record of **completing projects** on time and on budget?

▲ Is the developer **financially sound?**

▲ At the **handover**, are the building and unit constructed, finished and equipped as specified in the contract?

▲ Is there anything **incongruous** or unusual about the developer, salesperson, building site, contract, marketing materials, etc.?

▲ Is the developer facing **lawsuits** from unpaid suppliers and unhappy customers?

▲ What is the **payment schedule?**

⊿ Does the developer have all of the required **permits** and permissions?

⊿ When will you take **possession** of the property?

⊿ Have the developer's **previous projects** aged well?

⊿ How long is the developer's **warranty** and what is covered?

Prepurchase inspection

⊿ Do the **air conditioners** work? How old are they? What refrigerant do they use?

⊿ Is **aluminum wiring** installed in the home or building?

⊿ Has an **asbestos** survey been conducted?

⊿ Is corrosion visible on the **balcony** ironwork? Are there missing tiles or grout, signs of accumulated water or blocked drains?

⊿ Are the built-in **cabinets** complete? Is all of the hardware present and functional? Do the doors and drawers open smoothly? Is the finish free of blemishes?

⊿ Are the **ceilings** flat and free from water stains, mold, gaps and cracks?

⊿ Are the kitchen **counters** level and free from scratches and other defects?

⊿ Do the **doors** close smoothly? Is there insect damage or gaps between the door and the frame? Is the finish acceptable and the hardware intact and functional?

⊿ Do the switches, **electrical** outlets and lights work? Are there scorch marks on the outlets? Are the circuits on the breaker panel labeled correctly? Does the unit have modern, three-blade (BS 1363) outlets?

▲ Are the **floors** level? Are there gaps between the planks? Is water or insect damage visible?

▲ Is **galvanized steel pipe** present?

▲ Are the **gas** pipes or gas meter damaged?

▲ Are **plastered** and painted surfaces flat and free from cracks, mold, water stains and bulges?

▲ Does water flow smoothly through the **plumbing**, including the kitchen sink, floor drains and the sink, toilet and bathtub in the bathroom? Are there foul smells coming from the drains? Do the taps work?

▲ Has the unit been tested for **radon?**

▲ After an electrical **renovation**, has the contractor issued a WR1 or WR1(A) form? After a minor works project, has the contractor filed a MW02, MW04 or MW05 form with the Buildings Department?

▲ Does the **roof** leak?

▲ Has the unit been inspected for **termites** and other pests?

▲ Are **tiled** surfaces flat? Are tiles set straight and free from excess grout?

▲ Does the building have any **unauthorized building works?**

▲ Has the **water** been tested for excessive levels of lead?

▲ Do **windows** and sliding doors open smoothly? Are the frames anchored solidly? Is the glass clear and free from chips and inclusions? Are water stains visible nearby?

Income properties

▲ How much is the management company's **fee?**

▲ What is the tenant's payment **history?**

▲ How will I receive rental **income?**

▲ How much time remains on the tenant's **lease?**

▲ How much does the management company charge to **recruit** tenants?

▲ Is the **rent** in line with market rates?

▲ How does the management company **report** its activities?

▲ What **services** does the management company provide?

▲ Is the property **tenanted?**

▲ What is the rental **yield** or capitalization rate?

Neighborhood

▲ Are sources of **air pollution** or bad smells nearby?

▲ Is the neighborhood near a **brownfield** site or other source of soil pollution?

▲ Are nearby properties being **expropriated?**

▲ Is the neighborhood stable, decaying or being **gentrified?**

▲ Is **infrastructure** being built or demolished nearby?

▲ Is the relationship between the **rural committee** and residents cordial?

▲ Does the area have access to normal **services**: ambulance, broadband Internet, cable TV, electricity, fire department, piped gas, police, public transportation, mail, restaurants, schools, sewerage, shopping, telephone and water?

▲ Is the area at risk from **storm surges** or floods?

▲ Are there **transportation** concerns, such as a reliance on ferries, private roads or restrictions on the use of private vehicles?

▲ Are **undesirable neighbors** nearby, such as cemeteries, late-night entertainment, expressways, factories, incinerators or prisons?

Suppliers and contractors

▲ Are the vendor's **charges** competitive?

▲ Are there outstanding **complaints** or lawsuits against the vendor?

▲ Is the contractor **experienced** with your type of project?

▲ Does the supplier have professional indemnity, public liability and workers' compensation **insurance?**

▲ Have you obtained and checked the supplier's **references**?

▲ Is the supplier **registered** with the Minor Works Control Scheme or other government body or program?

▲ What **warranties** does the supplier offer on its products and services?

Title and transaction

▲ Are the management fees, rates or utilities in **arrears?**

▲ What are the estimated **closing costs?**

▲ Are there liens or **encumbrances** on the property?

▲ What decorations, appliances or **equipment** are included in the sale?

▲ Does the owners' corporation have sufficient funds in the bank account to cover **expenses** and major repairs?

- When is the **handover** date?

- Does the vendor have **negative equity** in the property?

- Is the property **price** consistent with the market valuation?

- Is the **vendor** the registered owner of the property? Is the vendor's identification in order?

INFORMATION SOURCES

This chapter features resources to help you buy and own property in Hong Kong. The entries are arranged alphabetically and, unless otherwise noted, are in English. Several useful books are also included in this section.

The inclusion or omission of a company should not be taken as a recommendation that you use or avoid them. Government and supranational organizations with an interest in housing and real estate are included. Additional information about entries marked with an asterisk can be found in the Government section.

Finally, things change quickly. Consider this information a starting point, not the last word.

Air pollution*

The Hedley Environmental Index, which is maintained by the School of Public Health at the University of Hong Kong, provides real-time data about Hong Kong's air quality. The index uses data from several monitoring stations to display information about suspended particulates, nitrogen dioxide, sulfur dioxide and ozone (http://hedleyindex.sph.hku.hk).

Alternative investments

In addition to owning physical property, there are several ways to gain exposure to Hong Kong real estate. You can:

▲ Buy shares in the developers listed below. Many of these companies are listed on the Hong Kong stock exchange (www.hkex.com.hk).

▲ Invest in a Hong Kong–focused real estate investment trust, such as Champion REIT (www.championreit.com), Fortune REIT (www.fortunereit.com), the Link REIT (www.thelinkreit.com), Prosperity REIT (www.prosperityreit.com), Regal REIT (www.regalreit.com) or Sunlight REIT (www.sunlightreit.com), that is listed on the Hong Kong stock exchange.

▲ Purchase shares in an exchange-traded fund, such as the Lippo
Select HK & Mainland Property ETF (http://lippoetf.com).

Appraisal services

See Surveyors, below.

Architects and designers

The Hong Kong Institute of Architects' Website offers a members directory and other resources (www.hkia.net).

The Royal Institute of British Architects (www.architecture.com) and
the American Institute of Architects (www.aiahk.org) have branches
in Hong Kong.

The Hong Kong Interior Design Association's Website includes a
members directory (www.hkida.org).

Commentary and analysis

Hong Kong has numerous think tanks and foundations, including
Civic Exchange (www.civic-exchange.org) and Designing Hong Kong
(www.designinghongkong.com), that produce useful research about
topics ranging from urban planning to pollution.

Hemlock (http://biglychee.com) is a blog run by an anonymous British
expatriate who has lived in Hong Kong for several decades. The blog
offers cynical, uncensored and often amusing commentary about politics and economics in Hong Kong.

The *South China Morning Post* (www.scmp.com) publishes regular col-
umns by Jake van der Kamp, a former business reporter and investment analyst.

Webb-site (http://webb-site.com) is operated by David M. Webb, a former investment banker who has lived in Hong Kong since 1991. Webb
provides independent opinions on Hong Kong topics, including business, finance, investment and legal and regulatory affairs.

Death*

Lists of *hongza*, or calamity homes, can be found on *Square Foot* magazine's Website (www.squarefoot.com.hk) and at www.hk-compass.com (Chinese only).

Developers

The Hong Kong Housing Society is an independent, not-for-profit organization that builds and manages subsidized and non-subsidized housing (www.hkhs.com).

The Real Estate Developers Association of Hong Kong is a trade body for the city's builders (www.reda.hk). The association's Website includes papers and background about development-related issues.

The following companies develop property in Hong Kong.

▲ Central Development (www.central-development.com)

▲ Cheung Kong Property Holdings (www.ckph.com.hk)

▲ China Overseas Holdings (www.cohl.com)

▲ Chinachem Group (www.chinachemgroup.hk)

▲ Chinese Estates Group (www.chineseestates.com)

▲ Emperor International Holdings (www.emperorint.com)

▲ Great Eagle Holdings (www.greateagle.com.hk)

▲ Hang Lung Properties (www.hanglung.com)

▲ Henderson Land Development (www.hld.com)

▲ HKR International (www.hkri.com)

▲ Hong Kong Ferry (Holdings) (www.hkf.com)

▲ Hongkong Land (www.hkland.com)

▲ Hopewell Holdings (www.hopewellholdings.com)

▲ Hysan Development (www.hysan.com.hk)

▲ K. Wah Group (www.luichewoo.com.hk)

▲ Kerry Properties (www.kerryprops.com)

▲ Lai Sun Group (www.laisun.com)

▲ MTR Corporation (www.mtr.com.hk)

▲ Nan Fung Group (www.nanfung.com)

▲ New World Development (www.nwd.com.hk)

▲ SEA Holdings (www.seagroup.com.hk)

▲ Shun Tak Holdings (www.shuntakgroup.com)

▲ Sino Group (www.sino.com)

▲ Sun Hung Kai Properties (www.shkp.com)

▲ Swire Properties (www.swireproperties.com)

▲ The Wharf (Holdings) (www.wharfholdings.com)

▲ Wheelock Properties (Hong Kong)
(www.wheelockpropertieshk.com)

Energy conservation*

In 2008, the Hong Kong government introduced the Energy Efficiency (Labeling of Products) Ordinance (Cap. 598). Under the law, new air conditioners, washing machines, refrigerators, compact fluorescent lights and dehumidifiers must carry a tag stating their energy consumption and efficiency rating (www.energylabel.emsd.gov.hk).

The Hong Kong Green Building Council Limited (HKGBC) is a non-profit organization that promotes the development of sustainable buildings (www.hkgbc.org.hk). The HKGBC is a member of the World Green Building Council (www.worldgbc.org).

Environmental resources*

The United States Environmental Protection Agency has information about indoor air quality, volatile organic compounds and other environmental issues (www.epa.gov).

The World Health Organization offers background information and data about environmental health issues (www.who.int/topics/environmental_health).

Financing*

Lenders
Hong Kong has an open and relatively free banking sector, which is overseen by the Hong Kong Monetary Authority. The authority's Website includes a list of banks (called authorized institutions and local representative offices) that is updated regularly.

The following lenders offer mortgages on Hong Kong properties.

▲ Agricultural Bank of China (www.hk.abchina.com)

▲ ANZ (www.anz.com)

▲ Bank of China (www.bochk.com)

▲ Bank of Communications (www.bankcomm.com.hk)

▲ Bank of East Asia (www.hkbea.com)

▲ China CITIC Bank International (www.cncbinternational.com)

▲ China Construction Bank (www.hk.ccb.com)

▲ Chiyu Banking Corp. (www.chiyubank.com)

▲ Chong Hing Bank (www.chbank.com)

▲ Citibank (www.citibank.com.hk)

▲ Dah Sing Bank (www.dahsing.com)

▲ DBS (www.dbs.com.hk)

▲ Fubon Bank (www.fubonbank.com.hk)

▲ Hang Seng Bank (http://bank.hangseng.com)

▲ HSBC (www.hsbc.com.hk)

▲ ICBC (www.icbcasia.com)

▲ Nanyang Commercial Bank (www.ncb.com.hk)

▲ OCBC Wing Hang Bank (www.ocbcwhhk.com)

▲ Orix Asia (www.orix.com.hk)

▲ Public Bank (Hong Kong) (www.publicbank.com.hk)

▲ Shanghai Commercial Bank (www.shacombank.com)

▲ Standard Chartered (www.sc.com)

▲ United Overseas Bank (www.uobgroup.com)

▲ Wing Lung Bank (www.winglungbank.com)

Mortgage brokers
▲ Centaline Mortgage Broker (www.centamortgage.com)

▲ Lifestyle Brokers (www.lfsbrokers.com)

▲ mReferral (www.mreferral.com)

Mortgage insurance

Mortgage insurance—which allows a borrower to increase her loan-to-value ratio—is available from The Hong Kong Mortgage Corporation (www.hkmc.com.hk). In addition to the government-owned HKMC, mortgage insurance is provided by private sector companies, such as QBE Mortgage Insurance (Asia) (www.qbemiasia.com).

Reverse mortgages

The Hong Kong Mortgage Corporation partners with local banks to offer reverse mortgages to Hong Kong identity card holders aged 55 and above.

Fire*

The U.S. Fire Administration has tips for preventing and surviving residential fires, including information for children, the elderly and people with disabilities (www.usfa.fema.gov).

For sale by owner (FSBO)

The FSBO culture that has taken root in Canada, the United States, the United Kingdom and elsewhere has not caught on in Hong Kong. Classified advertising sites like Geoexpat (www.geoexpat.com) have some listings, but the volumes are small.

Government

The Government of the Hong Kong Special Administrative Region operates an information portal (www.gov.hk) that is complemented by the 1823 telephone inquiry hotline.

- ▲ The **Appeal Board Panel (Town Planning)** is a forum for challenging decisions made by the Town Planning Board (www.devb.gov.hk/tpab).

- ▲ The **Buildings Department's** Website has information about maintenance, water leaks, unauthorized building works and the Minor Works Control System. The access to information section includes lists of accredited architects, engineers and surveyors as well as general, specialist and minor works contractors (www.bd.gov.hk). Building plans can be checked at https://bravo.bd.gov.hk.

▲ The **Census and Statistics Department** collects data on property, housing, population and other subjects (www.censtatd.gov.hk).

▲ The **Civil Engineering and Development Department's** Website includes information about landslides and slope maintenance (www.cedd.gov.hk).

▲ The **Companies Registry** collects information on companies that are incorporated in Hong Kong (www.cr.gov.hk).

▲ The **Consumer Council** is a public advocate for consumer interests (www.consumer.org.hk).

▲ The **Drainage Services Department** is responsible for flood prevention and for Hong Kong's sewerage system (www.dsd.gov.hk).

▲ The **Education Bureau's** Website has lists of local and international schools (www.edb.gov.hk).

▲ The **Electrical and Mechanical Services Department** sets safety and efficiency standards for a range of products (www.emsd.gov.hk).

▲ The **Environmental Protection Department** coordinates and carries out pollution prevention and control activities (www.epd.gov.hk).

▲ The **Estate Agents Authority** regulates real estate agents and agencies. The authority's Website includes resources for people buying and selling homes (www.eaa.org.hk).

▲ The **Fire Services Department** provides fire-fighting and ambulance services. The department's Website includes fire safety information and a list of approved fire equipment contractors (www.hkfsd.gov.hk).

▲ The **Food and Environmental Hygiene Department's** Website includes information about rats, mosquitoes and other pests that are common in Hong Kong. The department also manages the city's public cemeteries and crematoria (www.fehd.gov.hk).

▲ The **Home Affairs Department** has a diverse portfolio that includes encouraging the formation of owners' corporations for buildings and licensing hotels and guesthouses (www.had.gov.hk).

▲ The **Hong Kong Housing Authority** develops and implements Hong Kong's public housing program (www.housingauthority.gov.hk).

▲ The **Hong Kong Map Service** offers a range of maps and aerial photographs (www.hkmapservice.gov.hk).

▲ The **Hong Kong Monetary Authority** supervises the city's financial system, including banks (www.hkma.gov.hk).

▲ The **Hong Kong Observatory** is the government's weather service. It also monitors background radiation levels, tsunamis and seismic activity (www.hko.gov.hk).

▲ The **Hong Kong Trade Development Council** promotes the city's traders, manufacturers and service providers and organizes exhibitions and trade shows (www.hktdc.com).

▲ The **Housing Managers Registration Board** catalogs and disciplines housing managers (www.hmregistration.org.hk).

▲ The **Independent Commission Against Corruption** fights bribery and similar crimes (www.icac.org.hk).

▲ The **Indoor Air Quality Information Center** has links to contractors, technical standards and other resources (www.iaq.gov.hk).

▲ The **Information Services Department** is the government's publisher and public relations service. It communicates policy statements and emergency announcements (www.isd.gov.hk)

▲ The **Inland Revenue Department** collects taxes (www.ird.gov.hk).

▲ The **Lands Department** is responsible for land valuation, land acquisition, estate management, land leases, surveys, map production, slope maintenance, approving the presale of uncompleted flats and deeds of mutual covenant (www.landsd.gov.hk).

▲ The **Land Registry** provides property registration and information services (www.landreg.gov.hk). The Integrated Registration Information System permits online searches of the Land Registry (www.iris.gov.hk).

▲ The **Lands Tribunal** hears cases about the possession of property; building management and deeds of mutual covenant; compensation payable as a result of expropriation; compulsory sale for redevelopment; and appeal cases relating to rates and government rent (www.judiciary.gov.hk).

▲ The **Office of the Commissioner of Insurance** supervises Hong Kong's insurance industry (www.oci.gov.hk).

▲ The **Office of the Communications Authority** oversees broadcasters and telecommunications companies (www.ofca.gov.hk).

▲ The **Office of the Ombudsman** investigates and rectifies government maladministration (www.ombudsman.hk).

▲ The **Rating and Valuation Department** assesses rates (property tax) and government rent, and provides advisory services on landlord and tenant matters (www.rvd.gov.hk). The department's Property Information Online service offers rates and valuation data for individual properties and market statistics (www.rvdpi.gov.hk).

▲ The **Sales of First-hand Residential Properties Authority** was established to ensure that the Residential Properties (First-hand Sales) Ordinance (Cap. 621) is implemented effectively (www.srpa.gov.hk). The authority also operates the Sales of First-hand Residential Properties Electronic Platform, an online database of sales brochures, price lists and transactions of new residential developments (www.srpe.gov.hk).

⬥ The **Small Claims Tribunal** handles matters, including debts and damage to property, valued at $50,000 and less (www.judiciary.gov. hk).

⬥ The **Town Planning Board** creates rural and urban plans, including approved building types (www.info.gov.hk/tpb). Interactive maps of outline zoning plans are available from www.ozp.tpb.gov. hk.

⬥ The **Urban Renewal Authority** redevelops old neighborhoods (www.ura.org.hk).

⬥ The **Water Supplies Department** supplies water to residential, commercial and institutional customers (www.wsd.gov.hk).

Home automation

Automation companies such as Crestron (www.crestron.com) and Lutron (www.lutron.com) have been joined in the home automation market by computer hardware and software firms, including Apple (www.apple.com), Google (www.google.com), Intel (www.intel.com), Microsoft (www.microsoft.com) and a growing number of start-ups. Amazon, meanwhile, has opened a home automation store (www. amazon.com).

Home inspection

The International Association of Certified Home Inspectors is a trade group for home inspectors. It has a chapter in Hong Kong (www.nachi. org). The association maintains a database showing the life expectancy of home components, including windows and air conditioners (www.nachi.org/life-expectancy.htm).

Infestation*

The National Pest Management Association's Website includes information about insects and other household pests, as well as links to exterminators in Hong Kong (www.pestworld.org).

The University of Florida's Entomology and Nematology Department has detailed information about termites and other insects (http://entomology.ifas.ufl.edu).

Insurance*

Hong Kong has several trade bodies for the insurance industry, including the Hong Kong Confederation of Insurance Brokers (www.hkcib.org), the Hong Kong Federation of Insurers (www.hkfi.org.hk), the Insurance Institute of Hong Kong (www.iihk.org.hk) and the Professional Insurance Brokers Association (www.piba.org.hk). Each group's Website includes a registry of members, industry data and other information.

The U.S.–based Insurance Information Institute offers an exhaustive glossary of insurance terms and other resources (www.iii.org).

In July 2013, the International Association of Insurance Supervisors published a list of global systemically important insurers, which are the world's largest insurance companies. Of the nine companies on the list, the following offer property and casualty insurance in Hong Kong and are a good starting point for home insurance.

- Allianz (www.allianz.com)

- American International Group (www.aig.com)

- Assicurazioni Generali (www.generali.com)

- Aviva (www.aviva.com)

- AXA (www.axa.com)

- Ping An Insurance (www.pingan.com)

- Prudential plc (www.prudential.co.uk)

International brands

Appliances and electronics

▲ Bang & Olufsen; audiovisual equipment (www.bang-olufsen.com)

▲ Bosch; appliances (www.bosch.com)

▲ Carrier; heating, ventilation and air-conditioning systems (www.carrier.com)

▲ Crestron; lighting and home automation systems (www.crestron.com)

▲ Electrolux; appliances (www.electrolux.com)

▲ Fisher & Paykel; appliances (www.fisherpaykel.com)

▲ Fujitsu; air-conditioning systems (www.fujitsu.com)

▲ Haier; appliances (www.haier.net)

▲ Hitachi; audiovisual equipment and appliances (www.hitachi.com)

▲ Leviton; lighting and home automation systems (www.leviton.com)

▲ LG; audiovisual equipment and air-conditioning systems (www.lg.com)

▲ Lutron; lighting and home automation systems (www.lutron.com)

▲ Miele; appliances (www.miele.com)

▲ Mitsubishi Electric; audiovisual equipment and appliances (www.mitsubishielectric.com)

▲ Panasonic; audiovisual equipment and appliances (www.panasonic.com)

▲ Philips; audiovisual equipment and appliances (www.philips.com)

▲ Samsung; audiovisual equipment and appliances (www.samsung.com)

▲ Sharp; audiovisual equipment and appliances (www.sharp-world.com)

▲ Siemens; appliances, lighting and home automation systems (www.siemens.com)

▲ Smeg; appliances (www.smeg.com)

▲ Sony; audiovisual equipment (www.sony.com)

▲ Toshiba; audiovisual equipment (www.toshiba.com)

Bathrooms and kitchens

▲ Blum; kitchen systems (www.blum.com)

▲ Boffi; kitchens and bathrooms (www.boffi.com)

▲ Bulthaup; kitchen systems (www.bulthaup.com)

▲ Duravit; sanitary ware (www.duravit.com)

▲ Gaggenau; kitchens and appliances (www.gaggenau.com)

▲ Hansgrohe; plumbing (www.hansgrohe.com)

▲ Kohler; sanitary ware (www.kohler.com)

▲ Leicht; kitchens (www.leicht.com)

▲ Moen; plumbing and sanitary ware (www.moen.com)

▲ Poggen Pohl; kitchens and appliances (www.poggenpohl.com)

▲ Snaidero; kitchens (www.snaidero.com)

▲ Sub-Zero/Wolf; kitchen appliances (www.subzero-wolf.com)

▲ Toto; sanitary ware (www.toto.com)

▲ Valcucine; kitchens (www.valcucine.com)

▲ Viking; appliances (www.vikingrange.com)

Floor and window coverings
▲ Armstrong; floor coverings (www.armstrong.com)

▲ Hunter Douglas; window coverings (www.hunterdouglas.com)

Furniture
▲ Armani Casa; furniture and accessories (www.armanicasa.com)

▲ Cassina; Le Corbusier and Frank Lloyd Wright furniture (www.cassina.com)

▲ Herman Miller; Eames and Aeron chairs (www.hermanmiller.com)

▲ Ikea; furniture and accessories (www.ikea.com)

▲ Ralph Lauren; furniture and accessories (www.ralphlauren.com)

▲ Versace; furniture and accessories (www.versace.com)

Law*

Hong Kong's laws can be found at www.legislation.gov.hk.

Arbitration in Hong Kong follows the rules set out by the United Nations Commission on International Trade Law (UNCITRAL). The Hong Kong Mediation Center (www.mediationcentre.org.hk) and the Hong Kong International Arbitration Center (http://hkiac.org) offer dispute resolution services.

The Community Legal Information Center is a bilingual Website run by the Faculty of Law and the Department of Computer Science at the

University of Hong Kong. The site offers information in plain English about the local legal system, including property law (www.hkclic.org).

The Hong Kong Bar Association is a professional body for barristers. The association's Website includes lists of barristers, mediators and arbitrators (www.hkba.org).

The Law Society of Hong Kong's Website includes lists of accredited solicitors, law firms and reverse mortgage counselors as well as an explanation of the home buying process (www.hklawsoc.org.hk).

Land Administration and Practice in Hong Kong by Roger Nissim (Hong Kong University Press, 2012, ISBN: 978-988-80838-0-0) is written for a professional audience and contains a great deal of legal and technical information.

Property Law in Hong Kong: An Introductory Guide by Stephen Mau (Hong Kong University Press, 2014, ISBN: 978-988-82086-1-6) is an easy-to-read book written for general audiences.

Maps*

Map services by Google (http://maps.google.com) and Microsoft (www.bing.com/maps) offer street-level images that can be helpful if you are investigating a neighborhood.

Old Maps Online offers a range of historical maps of Hong Kong (www.oldmapsonline.org)

Media

Hong Kong
China Daily is a Mainland-owned newspaper that is published in Hong Kong (www.chinadaily.com.cn).

Radio Television Hong Kong's Radio 3 often covers real estate on its weekday morning talk shows (www.rthk.hk).

The *South China Morning Post* is a daily newspaper that publishes a real estate supplement on Wednesdays. On Sundays, *Post Magazine* features home renovations (www.scmp.com).

Square Foot is a biweekly, free magazine that includes real estate listings, articles and advice (www.squarefoot.com.hk).

The Standard is a free tabloid newspaper that publishes a real estate section on Thursdays (www.thestandard.com.hk).

TVB Pearl covers property on *The Pearl Report* and *Money Magazine* (www.tvb.com).

International

Major international newspapers, including the *Financial Times* (www.ft.com), the *International New York Times* (www.inyt.com) and *The Wall Street Journal* (www.wsj.com) report on Hong Kong property.

Hong Kong property is also covered by wire services such as Bloomberg (www.bloomberg.com) and Reuters (www.reuters.com). Yahoo! News compiles stories from wire services, including Reuters, Agence France-Presse and the Associated Press (http://news.yahoo.com).

The New Territories

Civic Exchange, a Hong Kong think tank, published three reports that explain the Small House Policy and the realities of housing in the New Territories. Rethinking the Small House Policy (2003), Small House Policy II: An Update (2013) and Small Houses, Big Effects: Public Opinion Survey on the Small House Policy (2015) are available from www.civic-exchange.org.

The Purchase of a Village House in the New Territories is a guide published by the Hong Kong government (www.landsd.gov.hk/en/legco/purchas.htm).

The Heung Yee Kuk has a Website that was dormant when this book went to press (www.heungyeekuk.org).

Myself a Mandarin is a memoir by Austin Coates, a British magistrate administering justice in the New Territories (Oxford University Press China, 1988, ISBN: 978-019 58419-9-2).

The Great Difference: Hong Kong's New Territories and Its People 1898-2004 by James Hayes (Hong Kong University Press, 2013, ISBN: 978-988-81397-5-0) is a thorough history of the New Territories.

Nuclear power*

The Hong Kong government maintains a contingency plan and reports on "operational events" at the Daya Bay reactors in Guangdong (www.dbcp.gov.hk). The Daya Bay Nuclear Power Operations and Management Company's Website includes information about the plants. Note that the English content on the site differs from the Chinese (www.dnmc.com.cn).

Information about nuclear power in China is available from the industry's trade body, the World Nuclear Association (www.world-nuclear.org).

Price information

Centaline publishes a monthly property price index called the Centa-City Index (http://hk.centadata.com/cci/cci_e.htm)

Property management*

The Hong Kong Association of Property Management Companies' Website includes a members list (www.hkapmc.org.hk).

Real estate agencies

The Hong Kong Real Estate Agents General Association is trade body for agents (www.hkreaga.org) (Chinese only).

The following list includes multinational companies, international franchises, large local agencies and a sampling of small boutique operations. Many of the following Websites include property listings.

▲ At Home in Hong Kong (www.athomeinhongkong.com)

▲ CBRE (www.cbre.com)

▲ Centaline (www.centanet.com)

▲ Century 21 (www.century21global.com)

▲ Chartersince (www.chartersince.com.hk)

▲ Colliers International (www.colliers.com)

▲ C S Property Agency (www.chungsen.com.hk)

▲ Cushman & Wakefield (www.cushmanwakefield.com)

▲ Engel and Voelkers (www.engelvoelkers.com)

▲ Executive Homes (www.executivehomeshk.com)

▲ Habitat Property (http://habitat-property.com)

▲ Hong Kong Homes (www.hongkonghomes.com)

▲ Hong Kong Property (www.hkp.com.hk)

▲ House Hunters (www.househunters.com.hk)

▲ Jones Lang LaSalle (www.jll.com)

▲ Knight Frank (www.knightfrank.com)

▲ Landmark Asia (www.landmarkasia.com)

▲ Landscope Christie's (www.landscope-christies.com)

▲ Midland Realty (www.midland.com.hk)

▲ Oasis Property (http://oasisproperty.com.hk)

▲ Qfang (http://hk.qfang.com) (Chinese only)

▲ Ricacorp Properties (www.ricacorp.com)

▲ Savills (www.savills.com)

▲ Sotheby's (www.sothebysrealty.com)

▲ Treasure Land (www.treasureland.com.hk)

▲ Unique Home (http://uniquehome.com.hk)

▲ Vigers (www.vigers.com)

Renovations*

Toolbase.org is a Website maintained by the National Association of Home Builders in the United States. While the site is written for an American audience, it has useful links and information about renovations, building and construction techniques, energy efficiency, universal design and other topics (www.toolbase.org).

Research and statistics

Financial institutions
Financial institutions produce research that usually falls into two categories: macroeconomic analysis and reports on property developers as investment targets. You may need to be a client to obtain these reports.

▲ Barclays Bank (www.barclays.com)

▲ BNY Mellon (www.bnymellon.com)

▲ Citibank (www.citibank.com)

▲ CLSA (www.clsa.com)

▲ Credit Suisse (www.credit-suisse.com)

▲ Goldman Sachs (www.gs.com)

▲ HSBC (www.hsbc.com)

▲ J.P. Morgan (www.jpmorgan.com)

▲ Merrill Lynch (www.ml.com)

▲ Morgan Stanley (www.ms.com)

▲ Royal Bank of Scotland (www.rbs.com)

▲ Standard Chartered (www.sc.com)

▲ UBS (www.ubs.com)

Institutes and others

Credit rating agencies, including Fitch (www.fitchratings.com), Moody's (www.moodys.com) and Standard & Poor's (www.standardandpoors.com) provide a range of research and data.

The Economist Intelligence Unit produces a range of paid and free research (www.eiu.com).

McKinsey & Company is a management consultancy that produces articles and research on a range of property-related topics (www.mckinsey.com).

The Urban Land Institute is a U.S.–based nonprofit organization that conducts research and publishes materials on real estate-related topics around the world (www.uli.org).

Real estate agencies

The multinational real estate agencies listed above produce research material. While much of the material is written for investors and corporate end-users, it can be a good source of information about market conditions and emerging trends. Some sites require registration.

Software

Architecture and design
Design software comes in three variations. The first is professional computer-aided design (CAD) software, like the packages sold by Autodesk (http://autodesk.com). This software is powerful and has a steep learning curve, which may be hard to justify if you are only involved in one or two projects. Autodesk also offers software rental plans, free viewers and mobile apps, and a free Web-based program called Homestyler (www.homestyler.com) that lets you create floor plans in two and three dimensions.

Second is consumer-oriented software from IMSI/Design (www.imsidesign.com), Punch! Software (www.punchsoftware.com) and others. Software in this category is less expensive, less sophisticated and easier to learn than professional products. Android and iOS versions are available for use on tablets.

Third is free software like Sketchup, a versatile, three-dimensional modeling package. A basic version of Sketchup is free for computers using the Windows or Mac operating systems. A professional version and video tutorials are also available (www.sketchup.com).

Floorplanner is a Web-based design tool that lets you create two- and three-dimensional room layouts and home designs (www.floorplanner.com). The basic program is free; a premium, paid service provides extra functionality. Sweethome (www.sweethome3d.com) is an open-source program that is similar to Floorplanner and available in 24 languages. Ikea offers online design tools that may be useful if you are planning to use that company's furniture (www.ikea.com).

Decoration
The Internet is a useful source of tools for generating color schemes. Paint manufacturers such as Dow Chemical operate sites with tools to help you choose a color theme (www.paintquality.com). Intended primarily for Web designers, Colorotate includes useful tools for understanding and working with color (www.colorotate.com).

Kuler lets you build color schemes and send color information to other Adobe products, such as Illustrator, InDesign and Photoshop (http://kuler.adobe.com). Colr.org is similar to Kuler, but easier to use (www.colr.org).

Colorjive lets you upload a photo of a room and virtually "paint" it. A premium version, which allows you to store images online, is also available (http://colorjive.com).

The myhomeideas blog has a calculator that lets you enter the dimensions of a room and determine how much paint, carpet or tile you'll need (www.myhomeideas.com/project-calculator).

Pinterest (www.pinterest.com) can be useful for inspiration, as can Houzz (www.houzz.com). Zillow Digs lets you see decoration ideas sorted by room, color scheme, price range and popularity (www.zillow.com/digs).

Surveyors*

The Hong Kong Institution of Surveyors' Website includes a list of land surveyors (www.hkis.org.hk).

The Royal Institution of Chartered Surveyors, a trade group that includes land surveyors as well as other property, land and construction professionals, has a Hong Kong chapter (www.rics.org).

Tax*

The Hong Kong Institute of Certified Public Accountants' Website includes a directory of members (www.hkicpa.org.hk).

Large accounting firms, including Deloitte (www.deloitte.com), Ernst & Young (www.ey.com), Grant Thornton (www.grantthornton.com), KPMG (www.kpmg.com) and PricewaterhouseCoopers (www.pwc.com), produce free real estate guides and bulletins containing useful information about local tax and accounting issues. These firms also produce tax guides for expatriates.

Translation

Google Translate lets you enter a word, a paragraph or an entire Website, which it then translates. While the site is no substitute for a professional translator, it will give you a general idea of the original text's meaning. It's fast, free and integrated with Google's Chrome browser (www.translate.google.com).

The Multilingual Interpreters and Translators Association is an independent body for interpreters and translators in Hong Kong (http://mitahk.org).

Universal design

Buildings that incorporate universal design are aesthetically pleasing and usable by the greatest number of people possible, regardless of their age or ability.

The Center for Universal Design at NC State University's College of Design has information for people who are building or renovating a home, including floor plans, checklists and design suggestions (www.ncsu.edu/ncsu/design/cud).

A Practical Guide to Universal Home Design is available from the Iowa Program for Assistive Technology (www.iowaat.org/udbooklet).

Utilities*

Electricity
CLP Power supplies electricity to customers in Kowloon, the New Territories and all of the outlying islands, except Lamma (www.clp.com.hk).

Hong Kong Electric supplies electricity to customers on Hong Kong Island and Lamma (www.hkelectric.com).

Gas
Hong Kong and China Gas , which is also known as Towngas, supplies gas to customers throughout Hong Kong (www.hkcg.com).

Telecommunications

Hong Kong Broadband Network offers residential telephone, IDD, Internet and cable TV services (www.hkbn.net).

Hong Kong Cable Television offers residential telephone, cable TV and Internet services (www.cabletv.com.hk).

Hutchison Global Communications offers Internet and residential, mobile and IDD telephone services (www.hgc.com.hk).

New World Telecommunications offers residential telephone, IDD and Internet services (www.newworldtel.com).

PCCW provides residential, mobile and IDD telephone as well as Internet and cable TV services (www.pccw.com).

Weather*

Tropical Storm Risk combines the efforts of the British Meteorological Office and several insurance and reinsurance companies to map and predict the progress of storms worldwide (www.tropicalstormrisk. com).

The U.S.–based Cooperative Institute for Meteorological Satellite Studies offers a similar service (http://cimss.ssec.wisc.edu/tropic2).

NOTES

The Buying Process

1. "Sale & Purchase of Property (Real Estate)," Community Legal Information Center, 2015.

2. "Guide on How to Invest in Real Estate in Hong Kong," Mayer Brown JSM, 2012.

3. "Purchase of Residential Premises," Law Society of Hong Kong, August 2014.

Real Estate Agents

1. "Types of Licenses," Estate Agents Authority, 2011.

2. "Licensing Requirements," Estate Agents Authority, 2011.

3. "Frequently Asked Questions," Estate Agents Authority, 2011.

Ownership and Property Rights

1. "Land Sale Records 2014/2015," Lands Department, Government of Hong Kong, July 8, 2015.

2. Roger Nissim, *Land Administration and Practice in Hong Kong*, 3rd ed., Hong Kong University Press, 2008, 38.

3. Danny Gittings, "What Will Happen to Hong Kong after 2047?," Social Science Research Network, October 1, 2011, 4.

4. Stephen Mau, *Property Law in Hong Kong: An Introductory Guide*, 2nd ed., Hong Kong University Press, 2014, 144.

Building Management

1. "Deed of Mutual Covenant and Owners' Corporation," Community Legal Information Center, 2012.

2. Yung Yau, "Willingness to Participate in Collective Action: The Case of Multiowned Housing Management," *Journal of Urban Affairs* 35, no. 2, May 2013, 153–71.

3. "Code of Practice on Building Management & Maintenance," Secretary for Home Affairs, Government of Hong Kong, 2007.

4. "Building Maintenance Guidebook," Buildings Department, Government of Hong Kong, 2002, 158.

5. Mats Wilhelmsson, "House Price Depreciation Rates and Level of Maintenance," *Journal of Housing Economics* 17, no. 1, March 2008, 88–101.

6. "Mandatory Building Inspection Scheme and Mandatory Window Inspection Scheme," Buildings Department, Government of Hong Kong, October 13, 2014.

7. "Hong Kong Flat Owners Face Hefty Repair Bills, Surveyors' Institute Says," *South China Morning Post*, October 5, 2012.

8. Benjamin Robertson and Elaine Yau, "Beating the Bid-Riggers," *South China Morning Post*, September 15, 2014.

9. "Daily Operation of Building Management: Lifts," Home Affairs Department, Government of Hong Kong, July 7, 2014.

10. Geoffrey Chan, "Buildings Energy Efficiency Ordinance Now in Effect," Mondaq/Mayer Brown JSM, October 10, 2012.

11. "Daily Operation of Building Management: Fire Service Installations," Home Affairs Department, Government of Hong Kong, July 28, 2008.

12. "Layman's Guide to Slope Maintenance," Civil Engineering Department, Government of Hong Kong, 2013, 7–8.

13. "Fresh Water Plumbing Maintenance Guide," Water Supplies Department, Government of Hong Kong, November 2008.

Risk Factors

1. "CAN's Mid-Year Air Quality Review 2014," Clean Air Network Limited, July 17, 2014.

2. Emily Badger, "Your Neighborhood Significantly Influences the Air You Breathe," The Atlantic Cities, December 17, 2013.

3. "Asbestos Control," Environmental Protection Department, Government of Hong Kong, August 12, 2014.

4. "Hong Kong Property Review 2015," Rating and Valuation Department, Government of Hong Kong, April 2015, 16, 30, 48, 54.

5. Michelle Yun, "'Haunted Apartments' Go for Cheap in Hong Kong," Bloomberg, November 12, 2014.

6. Yuen-ting Yeung, "The Effect of Chinese Culture on the Implicit Value of Graveyard View in Hong Kong Residential Property Market," The University of Hong Kong, 2005, 108.

7. Olga Wong and Tony Cheung, "Legco to Discuss Falling Windows," *South China Morning Post*, October 25, 2012.

8. Joanna Chiu and Amy Nip, "Larvotto Developer Promises to Replace Defective Windows," *South China Morning Post*, October 11, 2012.

9. "Fatalities from Falling Objects," Social Indicators of Hong Kong, June 18, 2014.

10. "LCQ18: Figures on Objects Being Thrown from a Height," Government Information Services, Government of Hong Kong, November 25, 2009.

11. "Mandatory Building Inspection Scheme and Mandatory Window Inspection Scheme," Buildings Department, Government of Hong Kong, October 13, 2014.

12. "Daily Operation of Building Management," Home Affairs Department, Government of Hong Kong, 2012.

13. P.W. Li and Edwin S.T. Lai, "Short-Range Quantitative Precipitation Forecasting in Hong Kong," *Journal of Hydrology, Quantitative Precipitation Forecasting*, 288, no. 1–2, March 20, 2004, 189–209.

14. T.C. Lee and C.F. Wong, "Historical Storm Surges and Storm Surge Forecasting in Hong Kong," Hong Kong Observatory, Government of Hong Kong, October 2007.

15. Mo-po Chan, "Sustainable Flood Prevention," Secretary for Development, Development Bureau, Government of Hong Kong, April 25, 2014.

16. Priscilla Chiu, "Hong Kong's Experience in Operating the Currency Board System," Hong Kong Monetary Authority, 2001.

17. Michael Wong, "Disaster Averted as Wartime Bomb Detonated," *South China Morning Post*, March 19, 2000.

18. "Simple Guide to 'Dangerous Hillside Orders'," Geotechnical Engineering Office, Government of Hong Kong, March 2012.

19. Lilian Vrijmoed, "Are Molds in Indoor Environments a Concern?," Department of Biology & Chemistry, City University of Hong Kong, April 5, 2012.

20. Jagjit Singh, Chuck Yu and Tai Kim Jeong, "Building Pathology—Toxic Mold Remediation," *Indoor and Built Environment* 20, no. 1, February 2011, 36–46.

21. Charlotta Eriksson, "Cardiovascular and Metabolic Effects of Long-Term Traffic Noise Exposure," Karolinska Institutet, 2012.

22. C.L. Wong, W. Chau and L.W. Wong, "Environmental Noise and Community in Hong Kong," *Noise and Health* 4, no. 16, July 1, 2002, 65.

23. Andy Fan, "Noise Pollution by the Construction Industry in Hong Kong," *Environmental Policy and Law* 36, no. 3–4, 2006, 173.

24. "World Nuclear Power Reactors," World Nuclear Association, April 1, 2014.

25. "Frequently Asked Questions: Water Seepage Problem," Buildings Department, Government of Hong Kong, 2004.

26. Rita Yi Man Li, "The Internalization of Environmental Externalities Affecting Dwellings: A Review of Court Cases in Hong Kong," *Economic Affairs* 32, no. 2, June 1, 2012, 81–87.

27. "Land Utilization in Hong Kong," Planning Department, Government of Hong Kong, July 16, 2014.

28. "Housing in Figures 2014," Hong Kong Housing Authority, 2014.

29. Norman T.L. Chan, "The HKMA's Countercyclical Prudential Measures and Financial Stability," Hong Kong Monetary Authority, July 14, 2014.

30. "Housing in Figures 2014."

31. "Potential Environmental Impact Associated with Pulverized Fuel Ash," Environmental Protection Department, Government of Hong Kong, January 6, 2014.

32. Naureen Mahbub Rahman and Bliss L. Tracy, "Radon Control Systems in Existing and New Construction: A Review," *Radiation Protection Dosimetry* 135, no. 4, August 1, 2009, 243–55.

33. Natasha Khan, "Hong Kong Faces Severe School Place Shortage, Group Says," Bloomberg, April 2, 2014.

34. Siu-Kei Wong et al., "Sick Building Syndrome and Perceived Indoor Environmental Quality: A Survey of Apartment Buildings in Hong Kong," *Habitat International* 33, no. 4, October 2009, 463–71.

35. Xiao-san Luo, Shen Yu and Xiangdong Li, "Distribution, Availability and Sources of Trace Metals in Different Particle Size Fractions of Urban Soils in Hong Kong: Implications for Assessing the Risk to Human Health," *Environmental Pollution* 159, no. 5, May 2011, 1317–26.

36. Celine Siu-lan Lee, Xiangdong Li and Wenzhong Shi, "Metal Contamination in Urban, Suburban and Country Park Soils of Hong Kong: A Study Based on GIS and Multivariate Statistics," *Science of the Total Environment* 356, no. 1–3, March 1, 2006, 57, 55.

37. Yu Bon Man et al., "Mutagenicity and Genotoxicity of Hong Kong Soils Contaminated by Polycyclic Aromatic Hydrocarbons and Dioxins/furans," *Mutation Research/Genetic Toxicology and Environmental Mutagenesis* 752, no. 1–2, April 15, 2013, 47–56.

38. Brenda Natalia Lopez et al., "Major Pollutants in Soils of Abandoned Agricultural Land Contaminated by E-Waste Activities in Hong Kong," *Archives of Environmental Contamination and Toxicology* 61, no. 1, July 2011, 101–114.

39. Suzanna Tong and Kin Che Lam, "Home Sweet Home? A Case Study of Household Dust Contamination in Hong Kong," *Science of the Total Environment* 256, no. 2–3, July 10, 2000, 115–123.

40. Lawrence W.C. Lai and Daniel C.W. Ho, "Unauthorized Structures in a High-Rise, High-Density Environment: The Case of Hong Kong," *Property Management* 19, no. 2, May 1, 2001, 112–23.

41. Felix Chan, "Sales of Flats at Trouble-Hit Project Could Be Postponed," *South China Morning Post*, June 9, 2000.

42. Alex Lo, "40pc of Flats in Sinking Estate 'Show Signs of Damage'," *South China Morning Post*, November 1, 1999.

43. Ka Lung Chan, "Termites," *Pest Control Newsletter* 26, April 2012, 2.

44. Shing Kwong Cheng and Siu Kin Ethan Cheung, "Analysis of Building Materials Damageable by Termites in Hong Kong," *Proceedings of the 10th Pacific-Termite Research Group Conference*, February 26–27, 2014.

45. "What Are Unauthorized Building Works," Buildings Department, Government of Hong Kong, October 2011.

46. Olga Wong, "200,000 Village House Owners Face Warnings," *South China Morning Post*, December 30, 2012.

Demographics

1. "Demographic Trends in Hong Kong 1981–2011," Hong Kong Census and Statistics Department, Government of Hong Kong, 2012, 4, 5.

2. "2011 Census—Thematic Report: Ethnic Minorities," Census and Statistics Department, Government of Hong Kong, December 2012, 27.

3. "Population (Hong Kong: The Facts)," Government of Hong Kong, April 2015.

4. "Hong Kong Population Projections 2012–2041," Census and Statistics Department, Government of Hong Kong, July 2012.

5. "Hong Kong's Future Population and Manpower Needs to 2030," The Bauhinia Foundation, 2014, 10.

6. Yuki Huen, "Hong Kong's Population Policy," Legislative Council Secretariat, Government of Hong Kong, February 4, 2014.

7. John M. Carroll, *A Concise History of Hong Kong*, Rowman & Littlefield Publishers, 2007, 150.

8. Douglas Todd, "Hong Kong Immigrants Streaming out of Canada," *Vancouver Sun*, May 2013.

9. Olga Wong, "Retiring to the Mainland is Losing its Luster for Hong Kong Seniors," *South China Morning Post*, August 4, 2014.

10. "Projections of Population Distribution 2013–2021," Planning Department, Government of Hong Kong, March 22, 2013, 8–11.

11. "Immigration (Hong Kong: The Facts)," Government of Hong Kong, September 2014.

12. "Immigration to Hong Kong for Non-Residents (Family Members)," Community Legal Information Center, 2015.

13. "Individual Visit Scheme Research Brief," Legislative Council Secretariat, Government of Hong Kong, 2014, 7.

Off The Plan

1. "LCQ8: System for the Pre-Sale of Uncompleted Residential Flats," Government Information Services, Government of Hong Kong, July 2, 2003.

2. "Data and Statistics," Sales of First-Hand Residential Properties Authority, August 12, 2015.

3. Alan T.S. Yip, "New Practice Note on Sale of First-Hand Residential Properties in Hong Kong," Mondaq/Mayer Brown JSM, May 5, 2015.

4. "Notes to Purchasers of First-Hand Residential Properties," Sales of First-hand Residential Properties Authority, April 2014, 12.

5. "Things to Know about Purchasing First-Hand Residential Properties," Gov.HK, Government of Hong Kong, March 2015.

6. "Notes to Purchasers of First-Hand Residential Properties," 15.

7. Roger Nissim, *Land Administration and Practice in Hong Kong*, 3rd ed., Hong Kong University Press, 2008, 62.

8. Residential Properties (First-Hand Sales) Ordinance, Cap. 621, 2013, sec. 2.

9. Sandy Li, "SHKP in 3-Year Warranties for Homes," *South China Morning Post*, November 26, 2013.

10. "Guide to Prospective Homebuyers Care on Purchase, Take over & Fit out," Hong Kong Institution of Surveyors, 2013, 26.

The New Territories

1. "Beginning of Land History in Hong Kong," Department of Land Surveying and Geo-Informatics, The Hong Kong Polytechnic University, 2015.

2. Siu Keung Cheung, *Gender and Community Under British Colonialism: Emotion, Struggle and Politics in a Chinese Village*, Routledge, 2006, 21.

3. John M. Carroll, *A Concise History of Hong Kong*, Rowman & Littlefield Publishers, 2007, 70.

4. Roger Nissim, *Land Administration and Practice in Hong Kong*, 3rd ed., Hong Kong University Press, 2008, 25.

5. Cheung, *Gender and Community Under British Colonialism*, 26.

6. Christine Loh, "Functional Constituencies: A Unique Feature of the Hong Kong Legislative Council," Civic Exchange, 2006, 192.

7. Carroll, *A Concise History of Hong Kong*, 155.

8. Mandy Lao, "Small House Policy II: An Update," Civic Exchange, 2013, 15.

9. "Son Crowned as New Kuk King," *The Standard,* June 2, 2015.

10. Michael DeGolyer, "Small Houses, Big Effects: Public Opinion Survey on the Small House Policy (Full Report)," Civic Exchange, 2015, 2.

11. Lao, "Small House Policy II: An Update," 7.

12. Nissim, *Land Administration and Practice in Hong Kong,* 63.

13. Lisa Hopkinson and Mandy Lao, "Rethinking the Small House Policy," Civic Exchange, September 2003, 6.

14. Malcolm Merry, "Not Entirely Legal - Part 53," LexisNexis: Hong Kong Legal and Law Community, August 8, 2012.

15. Lao, "Small House Policy II: An Update," 11.

16. Olga Wong, "Non-Indigenous Villagers Lose out in Compensation for Loss of Their Homes," *South China Morning Post*, July 7, 2014.

17. Danny Mok, "Builder and 11 Villagers Accused of Defrauding Lands Department in 'Small-House' Scam," *South China Morning Post,* January 15, 2015.

18. Lao, "Small House Policy II: An Update," 17.

19. Nissim, *Land Administration and Practice in Hong Kong,* 130.

20. Malcolm Merry, "Not Entirely Legal - Part 54," LexisNexis: Hong Kong Legal and Law Community, September 5, 2012.

21. Mimi Brown, *Property Rates in Hong Kong - Assessment, Collection and Administration,* Rating and Valuation Department, Government of Hong Kong, 2013, 140.

22. Nissim, *Land Administration and Practice in Hong Kong,* 129.

23. Hopkinson and Lao, "Rethinking the Small House Policy," 6.

24. Olga Wong, "200,000 Village House Owners Face Warnings," *South China Morning Post*, December 30, 2012.

25. "New Towns, New Development Areas and Urban Developments (Hong Kong: The Facts)," Government of Hong Kong, December 2014.

26. "Project Details," Express Rail Link, 2013.

27. Nissim, *Land Administration and Practice in Hong Kong,* 19.

28. Ernest Kao, "No Entry: Villagers Bar Access to Lantau Bay over Environmental 'Conspiracy,'" *South China Morning Post*, August 4, 2014.

29. Chi-fai Cheung, "So Lo Pun Villagers Protest against Unfair Land Treatment," *South China Morning Post*, October 13, 2014.

30. Benjamin Robertson and Ernest Kao, "Sai Kung Construction Project Meets Fierce Opposition as Residents Allege 'Abuse of Small-House Policy,'" *South China Morning Post*, May 30, 2015.

31. Kevin Drew, "Greed Said to Be Throwing Feng Shui Off Balance," *The New York Times*, January 25, 2011.

32. Ernest Kao, "'Hundreds of Graves' Lying in Hong Kong's Country Parks and Green Belts," *South China Morning Post*, January 21, 2014.

33. Ernest Kao and Benjamin Robertson, "Residents of Clear Water Bay Village Told to Make 'Maintenance Payments' or Lose Road Access to Homes," *South China Morning Post*, January 12, 2015.

34. Chi-fai Cheung, "Villagers Hit Another Roadblock in Sai Kung Village," *South China Morning Post*, September 17, 2014.

35. Julie Chu, "Elderly Hong Kong Woman Wins Compensation after Rural Leader, Property Agent Try to Push Her off Own Farmland," *South China Morning Post*, April 10, 2015.

36. Ernest Kao, "New Territories Villagers Say They Never Intended Violence at Legco," *South China Morning Post*, June 19, 2014.

37. "Demarcation District Survey," Department of Land Surveying and Geo-Informatics, The Hong Kong Polytechnic University, 2015.

38. "The Purchase of a Village House in the New Territories," Lands Department, Government of Hong Kong, 1998.

Nonresidential Property

1. "Hong Kong Property Review 2015," Rating and Valuation Department, Government of Hong Kong, April 2015, 54.

Approvals and Permits

1. "Minor Works Control System," Buildings Department, Government of Hong Kong, October 2012.

2. Venna Cheng, "The Minor Works Control System," Mondaq/Mayer Brown JSM, January 28, 2011.

Local Considerations

1. "Ozone Layer Protection," Environmental Protection Department, Government of Hong Kong, December 17, 2013.

Mortgages

1. "Frequently Asked Questions—Banking Stability," Hong Kong Monetary Authority, April 24, 2015.

2. Henry Cheng, "Compliance with Existing Prudential Measures on Property Mortgage Lending," Hong Kong Monetary Authority, January 19, 2015.

Insurance

1. "Home Insurance: Look Out for the Excess and Exclusions," The Consumer Council, July 16, 2012.

Taxes and Fees

1. "Pearl Wisdom Limited Agrees with SFC to Unwind Sale of The Apex Horizon Hotel Units," Securities & Futures Commission of Hong Kong, May 13, 2013.

2. "Deduction for Home Loan Interest," GovHK, Government of Hong Kong, May 2014.

3. Hilary Cordell, "An Overview of Special Stamp Duty, Buyer's Stamp Duty and Ad Valorem Stamp Duty," Okay.com, August 14, 2014.

4. "Hong Kong Stamp Duty," PwC, 2014.

INDEX

To minimize duplication, the section headings but not the individual entries from the "Information Sources" chapter are included in this index. For example, the index entry for Ikea refers to the company's appearance on page 149. Ikea also appears in the International brands section of "Information Sources" on page 233.

ABOUT THE AUTHOR

Christopher Dillon is an award-winning writer and entrepreneur based in Hong Kong.

In 2002, he bought and renovated a floor in an office building in Hong Kong's Central business district. Since then, he has purchased and refurbished a luxury apartment on the west side of Hong Kong Island and transformed a derelict steam laundry into a multimedia studio.

That experience inspired four books: *Landed Hong Kong* (2008), *Landed Japan* (2010), *Landed China* (2013) and *Landed Global* (2014), which includes case studies and data from more than 110 countries and territories.

A native of Canada, Dillon lived in Tokyo from 1989 to 1992. He appears regularly in the international media, as both a contributor and a guest.

www.ingramcontent.com/pod-product-compliance
Lightning Source LLC
Chambersburg PA
CBHW061143220326
41599CB00025B/4340